WHO RULES?

Edited by Roger Kimball

Who Rules?

SOVEREIGNTY,

NATIONALISM,

and the

FATE OF FREEDOM

in the

TWENTY-FIRST

CENTURY

ENCOUNTER BOOKS   NEW YORK · LONDON

First American edition published in 2020 by Encounter Books,
an activity of Encounter for Culture and Education, Inc.,
a nonprofit, tax exempt corporation.
Encounter Books website address: www.encounterbooks.com

Manufactured in the United States and printed on
acid-free paper. The paper used in this publication meets
the minimum requirements of ANSI/NISO Z39.48–1992
(R 1997) (*Permanence of Paper*).

FIRST AMERICAN EDITION

LIBRARY OF CONGRESS CATALOGING-IN-PUBLICATION DATA

Names: Kimball, Roger, 1953- editor.
Title: Who rules? : sovereignty, nationalism, and the fate of freedom in
the 21st century / edited by Roger Kimball.
Description: First American edition. | New York : Encounter Books, 2020.
Includes bibliographical references and index.
Identifiers: LCCN 2020008126 (print) | LCCN 2020008127 (ebook)
ISBN 9781641771283 (cloth) | ISBN 9781641771290 (epub)
Subjects: LCSH: Sovereignty—Philosophy. | Liberty—Philosophy.
Classification: LCC JC327 .W48 2020 (print) | LCC JC327 (ebook)
DDC 20.1/501--dc23
LC record available at https://lccn.loc.gov/2020008126
LC ebook record available at https://lccn.loc.gov/2020008127

Table of Contents

◆

Introduction

ROGER KIMBALL

◆

A MONG THE EPIGRAPHS that preface his recent book *The Demon in Democracy: Totalitarian Temptations in Free Societies*, the Polish philosopher Ryszard Legutko features a famous bit from Tocqueville's *Democracy in America*:

> I think then that the species of oppression by which democratic nations are menaced is unlike anything which ever before existed in the world....I am trying myself to choose an expression which will accurately convey the whole of the idea I have formed of it, but in vain....I seek to trace the novel features under which despotism may appear in the world. The first thing that strikes the observation is an innumerable multitude of men all equal and alike, incessantly endeavoring to procure the petty and paltry pleasures with which they glut their lives....Above this race of men stands an immense and tutelary power, which takes upon itself alone to secure their gratifications, and to watch over their fate. That power is absolute, minute, regular, provident, and mild. It would be like the authority of a parent, if, like that authority, its object was to prepare men for manhood; but it seeks on the contrary to keep them in perpetual childhood: it is well content that the people should rejoice, provided they think of nothing but rejoicing.

It is interesting to note that the first part of this passage also serves as an epigraph for Jacob Talmon's classic *The Origins of To-*

talitarian Democracy, a book that figures below in James Pierson's essay on the evolution of the United States. Pierson traces the development of the country from a union of states (which is what the Founders had forged) into a nation in the modern sense under Lincoln's guidance, and then, in recent decades, into a nation besieged by the centrifugal forces of multiculturalism and identity politics.

Talmon, writing in the 1950s, makes a critical distinction between liberal and totalitarian democracies. The essential difference between the two, he writes, is in their "different attitudes to politics." The liberal approach "assumes politics to be a matter of trial and error"; it regards political systems as "pragmatic contrivances of human ingenuity and spontaneity." Furthermore, it also recognizes "a variety of levels of personal and collective endeavor, which are altogether outside the sphere of politics."

By contrast, the totalitarian version of democracy is "based upon the assumption of a sole and exclusive truth in politics." Talmon calls this "political Messianism." Readers of Norman Cohn's classic *The Pursuit of the Millennium* will be familiar with the concept (as indeed will readers of Karl Marx). The "messianic" quality can be seen partly in the totalizing aspect of the vision—it is meant to organize and control the whole of our lives—partly in the presumption that it is both 1. *inevitable* and 2. *morally superior* to what came before. "[I]t postulates," Talmon writes, "a preordained, harmonious and perfect scheme of things, to which men are irresistibly driven, and at which they are bound to arrive."

Communism was one form of political Messianism. The supposedly "post-historical" liberal consensus that Francis Fukuyama championed in *The End of History* is another, kinder, gentler form of utopian presumption. It is worth noting that Fukuyama's book figures as a cautionary marker in several of the essays that follow. Why? Because it is precisely that overweening liberal consensus—the increasingly bureaucratic and notably *illiberal* liberalism espoused by the administrative state—that we set out to challenge in this volume.

Talmon was onto something deep, I believe, when he identified "the paradox of freedom" as the recognition that freedom is unfree so long as it is wed to "an exclusive pattern of social existence, even if this pattern aims at the maximum of social justice and security." The key is this: Do we take "men as they are" and look to politics to work from there? Or do we insist upon treating men "as they were meant to be, and would be, given the proper conditions"?

The former describes the traditional, genuinely liberal view of freedom. The latter describes what Talmon calls "totalitarian democracy." A classic source for the latter view is Jean-Jacques Rousseau. In *The Social Contract*, Rousseau says that anyone who would "dare to undertake the institution of a government must think himself capable, as it were, of *changing human nature*" (my emphasis).

Contrast that hubristic ambition with James Madison's acknowledgment, in *Federalist* 10, that different men have different and competing interests and that the "first object" of government is to protect those differences and the "diversity in the faculties" whence they arise.

The real battle that has been joined—and it is a battle that is in the process of forging a great political realignment—is not between virtuous progressive knights riding the steeds of liberalism, on the one hand, and the atavistic forces of supposedly untutored darkness represented by "populism," on the other.

No, the real battle is between two views of liberty. One is a parochial view that affirms tradition, local affection, and the subordination of politics to the ordinary business of life. Chris Buskirk touches on this point in his essay below:

In response to the Marxist challenges America faced from communist imperialism, conservatives became over-dependent on ideology. But true conservatism is essentially much more practical. Its vitality comes from a view of life that recognizes the primacy of the family, the uniting power of religion, and the risks to both of expecting too much from politics. Protecting those two basic human institutions so that they are free to thrive and to act in their roles is the primary role of good government. There are, of course, other important functions of government, and whatever government does must be done well and with integrity, but that means eschewing utopian projects, focusing on what can be done well, and restoring a sense of obligation that places the wellbeing of American citizens above every other interest.

The other view of liberty is more ambitious but also more abstract. It seeks nothing less than to boost us all up to that plane of enlightenment from which all self-interested actions look petty, if not criminal, and through which mankind as a whole (but not, alas, individual men, who hardly matter in this calculus) may hope for whatever salvation secularism leavened by utilitarianism may provide. It is worth noting in this context that the seductive pressure of millenarian ideology also propels the curious spectacle of "woke" radicalism according to which everything is susceptible to the demands of what the journalist Gavin Haynes has called a "purity spiral." You can never be revolutionary enough, Comrade, or sufficiently Green, or fervid enough in your "anti-racism."

We are still in the opening sallies of the Great Realignment. Many old alliances are being broken, many new ones formed. I expect a lot of heat, and even more smoke. I hope that there will also be at least occasional flashes of light.

It was to encourage such flashes, while also attempting to dissipate some of the attendant heat and smoke, that *The New Criterion* joined with the Center for American Greatness to ponder the question "Sovereignty or Submission?" We took our conference's title from John Fonte's 2011 book, *Sovereignty or Submission: Will Americans Rule Themselves or Be Ruled by Others?* In his essay below, Fonte expands his purview to consider how such progressive entities as Freedom House and the National Endowment for Democracy have, in their efforts to "promote democracy" across the globe, promoted instead exactly the sort of administrative, top-down, essentially illiberal form of governance that writers like Tocqueville and Talmon warned about.

"Transnational progressivism" is Fonte's brilliant coinage to describe this anti-nationalist impulse that seeks to transfer political power and decision-making "from democratic nations to supranational authorities and institutions" such as the European Union, the United Nations, the World Bank, the International Monetary Fund, and kindred organizations ("judges from the European Court of Human Rights and the International Criminal Court; career officials in the U.S. State Department, the British Foreign Office, and the German Foreign Ministry; American CEOs of major global corporations; NGOs such as Amnesty International, Human Rights Watch, and Greenpeace"; etc., etc.). The true political ends of such elite enterprises are generally swaddled in emollient rhetoric about freedom and democracy. But Fonte uncovers some revelatory gems that speak candidly about what's really at stake. For example, Robert Kagan of the Brookings Institution put it with all possible clarity when he declared in 2008 that the "United States...should not oppose, but welcome a world of *pooled and diminished national sovereignty*." My emphasis. "Pooled and diminished national sovereignty." At least we know where we stand.

The question of sovereignty—of who governs—is at the center of all contemporary populist initiatives. It has been posed with increasing urgency as the bureaucratic burden of what has been called variously the "deep state" or administrative state has weighed more and more forcefully upon the political and social life of Western democracies.

The phenomenon is often identified with the election of Donald Trump in November 2016. But the political, moral, and social realities for which Trump was a symbol and a conduit both predated his candidacy and achieved independent reality in countries as disparate as the United Kingdom, Hungary, Italy, and Brazil.

The question of sovereignty was perhaps most dramatically posed in the United Kingdom. In June 2016, more Brits voted to leave the European Union and return sovereignty to Parliament than had ever voted for any initiative in the long history of Great Britain. Some seventeen million voted to leave the European Union and regain local responsibility for their own lives. It took more than three years for that promissory note to be cashed. The UK formally began its split from the EU at 11 p.m. GMT on 31 January 2020. Like the Battle of Waterloo according to the Duke of Wellington, it was a "near run thing." Prime Minister Boris Johnson promised that he would, deal or no deal, get Brexit done by the end of October 2019. He was stymied for months, as much by the established elites of his own party as by Labour. The process of emancipation had not proceeded far before it was interrupted by the advent of a new Chinese import, the novel coronavirus which swept all other news from the front page for months (until, that is, it was half-superseded by the extortionist Kabuki theater of "Black Lives Matter"). As I write, Europe and the United States both are still in a state of state-enforced semi-hibernation or "lockdown," an insidious flu-like respiratory virus having paralyzed their populations with fear and transported their governments with the tantalizing prospect of greater control over every aspect of life.

President Trump has often spoken about the issue of sovereignty. In his first speech to the United Nations' General Assembly in September 2017, he said to a startled roomful of diplomats that "we are renewing this founding principle of sovereignty."

> Our government's first duty is to its people, to our citizens—to serve their needs, to ensure their safety, to preserve their rights, and to defend their values. As President of the United States, I will always put America first, just like you, as the leaders of your countries will always, and should always, put your countries first.

All responsible leaders have an obligation to serve their own citizens, and the nation-state remains the best vehicle for elevating the human condition.

Perhaps the most disturbing aspect of that speech was the shocked horror that it provoked among the entrenched globalist establishment for whom the whole idea of nation-states and patriotic allegiance to one's country seems like a barbaric affront to common decency. Imagine, a President of the United States declaring his intention to foster the well-being and prosperity of his own citizens!

A second key question, and one related to the issue of sovereignty, concerns what Lincoln called "public sentiment": the widespread, almost taken-for-granted yet nonetheless palpable affirmation by a people of their national identity.

Trump's slogan "America First" instantly became an object of contempt, ridicule, and hatred to the Left, the NeverTrump Right, and the entrenched bureaucracy of the administrative state. But Angelo M. Codevilla is correct that, before the progressive movement that began with Woodrow Wilson, "labeling any proposal or point of view as 'America First' would have been meaningless" because it would have been redundant. What else would an American administration promulgate? From George Washington through Teddy Roosevelt, an assumption of "America first" was simply taken for granted. Indeed, the phrase, Codevilla notes, "may be the most succinct description of George Washington's statecraft." By telling his fellow citizens that "the name of American, which belongs to you, in your national capacity, must always exalt the just pride of Patriotism, more than any appellation," Washington articulated the essence of Trump's slogan *avant la lettre*.

Increasingly, the pillars of that consensus—the binding realities of family, religion, civic duty, and patriotic filiation—have faltered before the blandishments of the globalist juggernaut. I think that the English philosopher Roger Scruton was correct when he observed,

"Democracies owe their existence to national loyalties—the loyalties that are supposedly shared by government and opposition." One pressing question we face—one raised in several of the essays that follow—is whether we can any longer count on that supervening loyalty to unite us. For most of the contributors, I'd say, the prognosis is, while not despairing, decidedly gloomy.

One reason for the gloominess is what some observers have called the "criminalization of policy differences." Consider the extent to which the term "populism" has been weaponized as a negative epithet by the self-appointed elites. As I have noted elsewhere, if you are able to charge someone with populist sympathies you get, free and for nothing, both the imputation of demagoguery and what was famously derided as a "deplorable" and "irredeemable" cohort. "Populism," that is to say, is wielded less as a descriptive than as a *delegitimizing* term. The element of existential depreciation is almost palpable.

So is the element of condescension. Inseparable from the diagnosis of populism is the implication not just of incompetence but also of a crudity that is partly aesthetic and partly moral. Hence the curiously visceral distaste expressed by elite opinion for signs of populist sympathy. When Hillary Clinton charged that half of Donald Trump's supporters were an "irredeemable" "basket of deplorables," when Barack Obama castigated small-town Republican voters as "bitter" folk who "cling to guns or religion or antipathy to people who aren't like them or anti-immigrant sentiment or anti-trade sentiment," what they expressed was not disagreement but condescending revulsion.

The debate over the location of sovereignty—is it with the people affected or with unaccountable elites?—has played a large role in the rise of the phenomenon we describe as "populism" in the United States as well as in Europe. For one thing, the question of sovereignty stands behind the rebellion against the political correctness and moral meddlesomeness that are such conspicuous and disfiguring features of our increasingly bureaucratic society. The smothering, Tocquevillian blanket of regulatory excess has had a wide range of practical and economic effects, stifling entrepreneurship and making any sort of productive innovation difficult.

The issue of sovereignty also stands behind the debate over immigration. Indeed, no issue is more central to the question "Who governs?" than the question of a nation's borders and who gets to decide how a country defines its first-person plural: the "We" that makes us who we are as a people.

Throughout his 2016 campaign, Donald Trump promised to enforce America's immigration laws, to end so-called "sanctuary cities," which advertise themselves as safe havens for illegal aliens (though of course politicians in those cities do not call them "illegal aliens"), and to sharpen vetting procedures for people wishing to immigrate to America from countries known as sponsors of terrorism.

Behind the reaction to Trump's efforts at immigration reform are two very different concepts of the nation-state and world order. One view sees the world as a collection of independent sovereign countries that, although interacting with one another, regard the care, safety, and prosperity of their own citizens as their first obligation. This is the traditional view of the nation-state. It is also Donald Trump's view. It is what licenses his talk of putting "America First," a concept that, *pace* the anti-Trump media, has nothing to do with Charles Lindbergh's isolationist movement of the late 1930s and everything to do with fostering a healthy sense of national identity and purpose.

The alternative view regards the nation-state with suspicion as an atavistic form of political and social organization. The nation-state might still be a practical necessity, but, the argument goes, it is a regrettable necessity inasmuch as it retards mankind's emancipation from the parochial bonds of place and local allegiance. Ideally, according to this view, we are "citizens of the world," not particular countries, and our fundamental obligation is to all mankind. This of course is the progressive view, and it would be hard to overstate its influence.

It would also be hard to overstate its incoherence. A "citizen" (from *civis*) is by definition a person whose affiliation is with a *particular* place, a "*civitas*." A "world-citizen" is therefore an oxymoron—which does not, alas, mean that it is without adherents. As Victor Davis Hanson argues below, the "erosion of the citizen" is accelerating as the mere fact of residence is increasingly taken to be synonymous with "legal citizenship." Consequently, "those who happen to live within the borders of the United States (legally or not) increasingly enjoy almost all the same rights as those Americans who were born here or were naturalized."

Hanson underscores the curious double standard that is at work in the breakdown of citizenship and elevation of "mere residence" to the status of legal immunity. "The rationale of the sanctuary city," he notes "is not politically neutral or apparently applicable to issues other than illegal immigration."

> No sanctuary entity, for example, would support similar nullifications of federal law by conservatives should they declare particular red counties exempt from the federal Endangered Species Act, or their citizens not subject to federal handgun background checks.

Progressives argue that a globalist supra-national world—a world without borders—is a necessary condition for free trade. But the spirit of local control tempers the cosmopolitan project of a borderless world with a recognition that the nation-state has been the best guarantor not only of sovereignty but also of broadly shared prosperity. What we might call the *ideology* of free trade—the globalist aspiration to transcend the impediments of national identity and control—is an abstraction that principally benefits its architects. As President Trump has observed, trade that is not fair is not free.

In the end, what the political philosopher James Burnham anatomized as the "managerial revolution" is part of a larger progressive project. The aim of this project is partly to emancipate mankind from such traditional sources of self-definition as national identity, religious affiliation, and specific cultural rootedness. As Daniel McCarthy shows in his essay below, Burnham castigates this hypertrophied form of liberalism (again, the phrase "illiberal liberalism" seems apt) as "an ideology of suicide" that has insinuated itself into the center of Western culture. In Burnham's view, the primary function of such liberalism was to "permit Western civilization to be reconciled to dissolution," to view weakness, failure, even collapse not as a defeat but "as the transition to a new and higher order in which Mankind as a whole joins in a universal civilization that has risen above the parochial distinctions, divisions, and discriminations of the past."

That is part of the story. Burnham also notes the extent to which the progressive, managerial revolution seeks to perpetuate and aggrandize the apparatus that oversees the dissolution he diagnoses. In other words, the operation of the administrative state is not only an effort to extend a certain vision of the world, it is also an effort to consolidate political power. That is one reason its opposition to populist and nationalist initiatives is so ferocious. As Gavin Haynes observed in his discussion of "purity spirals," what we see is "a bidding war for morality turned into a proxy war for power."

The globalist alternative dangled before us is a version of utopia. But like the Wizard of Oz, it is all show and no substance. Or rather, the substance is an erosion of traditional sources of strength and identity together with an assault on the middle class and its "deplorable" values as an impediment to the realization of beatitude. Increasingly, as Hanson notes below (and as Joel Kotkin examines at length in his new book *The Coming of Neo-Feudalism: A Warning to the Global Middle Class*), Western societies are reverting to a species of bifurcated society in which a tiny group of elites rule over a docile but imperfectly contented mass. What happens when the engines of prosperity falter is anyone's guess. John O'Sullivan speaks below of the advent of "sacrificial utopia." Only someone innocent of the writings of Orwell, and the machinations of Communist despotism, will think that an ironical designation.

Pre- & Post-Citizens

VICTOR DAVIS HANSON

◆

A MERICANS CHERISH their citizenship. Yet they have all but
lost it. The erosion of the citizen is insidiously accelerating in
two quite different directions. It seems as if we are reverting to tribal
pre-citizenship, in the manner of clan allegiances in the centuries
before the rise of the Greek polis and the seventh-century-B.C. in-
vention of the concept of the citizen (*politês*). Or perhaps the better
comparison is to the fifth-century A.D., when northern nomadic ethnic bands crossed the Rhine and Danube and replaced the multira-
cially encompassing notion of "*civis Romanus sum*"—"I am a Roman
citizen"—with tribal loyalties to fellow Goths, Huns, or Vandals.

In particular, a regression to a state of pre-citizenship can be seen
in the conflation of mere residence with legal citizenship. Whether they feel particularly American or not, those who happen to live
within the borders of the United States (legally or not) increasingly
enjoy almost all the same rights as those Americans who were born
here or were naturalized. In addition, multiculturalism is retribalizing
America, in the manner of the fragmentation and evaporation of the
Roman Empire. Millions seem to owe their first loyalty to those who
share similar ethnic, racial, or religious affinities rather than to shared
citizenship, common traditions, and collective histories that transcend
race, creed, and clan. And the middle class, the classical foundation
for citizenship, is also eroding as a medieval society of lords and peas-
ants returns, especially in progressive states like California.

On the more privileged end, we are paradoxically entering an age

1

of post-citizenship. Our alleged elites, mostly on the two coasts, often prefer to envision themselves as "citizens of the world" and, consequently, see their Americanism as passé. They prefer to respect the authority and reputation of transnational organizations rather than American legislative bodies and jurisprudence. Certainly, the protocols of the European Union earn more respect from many members of our professional classes than does the U.S. Constitution's Second Amendment.

Moreover, many of the freedoms enshrined in the Bill of Rights have already been radically curtailed by our current "cancel culture," which is supported by the demons of social media, the administrative state, the courts, and popular culture. An individual citizen's right that is legally protected is often practically impossible to enjoy. More formally, there is a concentrated academic, legal, and legislative effort to alter the Constitution, or at least to jettison abruptly decades of American legal and political traditions in the name of equality and at the expense of freedom and liberty.

Currently there are over five hundred so-called "sanctuary cities" inside the United States, in which federal immigration law has been rendered all but null and void. In these cities and counties, those who have violated federal law and resided without legal sanction, who are then arrested and charged with crimes, are protected from federal immigration enforcement and are not subject to deportation. This current annulment is somewhat similar to the nullification crisis of 1832–33, when South Carolina arbitrarily declared federal tariff laws non-binding within its own state jurisdiction—before backing down under threat of force by President Andrew Jackson.

The rationale of the sanctuary city is not politically neutral or apparently applicable to issues other than illegal immigration. No sanctuary entity, for example, would support similar nullifications of federal law by conservatives should they declare particular red counties exempt from the federal Endangered Species Act, or their citizens not subject to federal handgun background checks.

Some twelve states now issue driver's licenses without much effort to check legal residence—and thereby come into conflict with federal laws governing necessary identification criteria to pass security checks before boarding U.S. airline flights—with the result that many such states must now issue super-"real" driver's licenses that require additional proof of U.S. citizenship or legal residence to obtain. When I taught at California State University, Fresno, one of the strangest experiences was hearing complaints from out-of-state U.S.-citizen students who paid three times the tuition of California-based non-citizen residents, most of them residing in California without legal status. Most states do not distinguish between residents and citizens in allotting social services.

Three centuries of gradually accumulated American jurisprudence, custom, and tradition had previously delineated important legal differences between the concepts of citizenship and residence, both legal and illegal. Only citizens and legal residents could live inside the borders of the United States indefinitely. As a practical matter, since the 1920s only citizens have been allowed to vote in local and national elections. And in 1952, the federal government mandated the possession of a U.S. passport to leave and enter the country without government permission.

Already two of those three pillars of citizenship have eroded. There are currently somewhere between eleven and twenty million illegal aliens residing in the United States without legal sanction. Some have been given amnesty and others de facto exemptions from deportation. The number is increasing. Also becoming more prevalent is the notion and practice that legal citizenship is not particularly necessary to live indefinitely inside the United States, to obtain legal identification, to qualify for state and federal social services, or to cross at will U.S. borders without legal permission.

Aside from the fact that state "motor-voter" laws—which tie voter registration to the possession of a driver's license—often are deliberately blurred or lax enough to allow ballot-registration forms to be sent to illegal aliens, non-citizens have also been given the rights in some jurisdictions to vote in a few municipal elections, a trend that is likewise accelerating. Illegal aliens legally can vote in local San Francisco school board elections, and a number of other cities have voted to follow suit. And the trend is gaining strength.

In other words, we are returning to nineteenth-century practices, when the westward expansion of the United States, coupled with commensurately small state populations, often meant that there were no enforceable borders. On the relatively empty frontiers, few cared to ascertain the legal status of residents. But whereas in the distant past demography explained legal laxity, today the explanation is politics—or, rather, the doctrine of radical equality of result that seeks to erode any discriminating criteria concerning those residing in the United States.

Salad-bowl multiculturalism has replaced melting-pot multiracialism. The reason why the former Harvard Law School professor Elizabeth Warren and the former University of Colorado professor Ward Churchill both faked Native-American identities was to find the easiest and quickest way to advance their respective careers. They correctly assumed that employers would favor, or be forced to favor, those who identified as "hyphenated Americans" in general, and in particular those with minority ancestry.

Over the last thirty years, but especially during the Obama years, the concept of affirmative action gradually gave way to the notion of "diversity." The former doctrine had originated as a means to "level the playing field" and give African-Americans an edge in college admissions and hiring on the theory that the toxic legacy of slavery and Jim Crow required such reparatory remedies.

But once affirmative action was extended to other minorities without the clear historical grievances of blacks, the floodgates of racial and ethnic preferences were open. Such an amorphous term as "Latino" or "Hispanic" could include rich South Americans or indeed Spanish immigrants, as well as recently arrived Mexican citizens who had never experienced any American discrimination by virtue of never having resided inside the United States at all.

Class as proof of disadvantage was largely forgotten—as if the children of Attorney General Eric Holder or Jay-Z were less privileged than the impoverished offspring of an unemployed white Appalachian coal miner. Given that many Hispanics were superficially indistinguishable from the white majority, some sought to add accents to their names or change to Spanish spellings (Johns rebranded as Juans), and to create hyphenated names, all in an effort to reestablish privileged minority status. How odd that whiteness was claimed to offer intrinsic advantages, even as millions of Americans were finding ways, even if superficially, not to be labeled as white. And yet privilege and advantage were precisely what an apparently too-white Elizabeth Warren sought with her constructed Native-American identity.

During the Obama administration, the notion of "diversity" de facto abolished the two former assumptions of affirmative action: proof of prior or ongoing discrimination and economic disparity. More practically, "diversity" redefined the American body politic. Those who were now "diverse" encompassed almost anyone who claimed to be not white, however that amorphous term was defined. Diverse now included wealthy Asians or Cubans, and a host of other groups heretofore not considered oppressed minorities. And the new diversity comprised nearly 30 percent of the population, with assumed historical complaints against the white majority—a new binary that sometimes required the resurrection of the pernicious "one-drop" rule of the Old South to maintain such a huge constituency. Those with one-quarter, one-eighth, or one-sixteenth non-white ancestry often applied as minorities for jobs and university admissions.

Previous cultural differences in language, food, fashion, art, and music had enriched American life, but as subsidiaries to, rather than replacements of, the core of American citizenship and tradition and history. Now, diversity offers entire parallel and separate anti-Constitutional paradigms. Some students have begun to be housed on campus in race-specific houses. Others can select their potential roommates on the basis of race. "Safe spaces" have been reserved for students on the basis of race or sexuality. Standards of proportional representation are applied to hiring and admissions, and "disparate impact" theories find insidious racism even without the supporting evidence of actual victims. As Heather Mac Donald wrote in *The New Criterion*'s November 2019 issue, Asian-American citizens certainly have fewer constitutional rights of due process and non-discrimination when applying to Ivy League schools than do Latino-Americans or African-Americans.

Since the American founding, citizenship also assumed an active independent voter to elect representatives and ensure that the rights of the Constitution were protected. The Founders saw citizenship as nearly synonymous with a vibrant middle class, which at the origin of America comprised mostly independent and autonomous small farmers—a theme prevalent in Thomas Jefferson's reflections on the Constitution and the works of Crèvecœur and Tocqueville. Yet this additional pillar of citizenship likewise is slowly being diminished, resulting in a pre-citizen landscape of two rather than three classes.

Small farmers are now all but nonexistent, but their middle status after the Industrial Revolution had been absorbed by blue-collar workers and suburban wage-earners. Buying a home, being able to meet a manageable mortgage payment, attending college without crushing debt, and enjoying upward mobility were all considered central to avoiding a two-dimensional medieval society. Yet by most benchmarks, the framework of the middle class is eroding, as evidenced by rising mortgage costs as a percentage of family budgets, $1.5 trillion in aggregate student debt, and, until 2018, stagnant family income and workers' wages.

The result has been the gradual expansion of a large underclass that looks to government for redistributive justice, and a much wealthier elite who never seem subject to the ramifications of their own progressive bromides. The shrinking middle, lacking the romance of the distant poor and the appropriate taste and culture of the rich, is often caricatured as greedy, materialist, and needing of instruction on race, class, and gender.

If the foundations of citizenship are being undermined, so too are its superstructures. Globalism started out with the spread of quasi-capitalism that introduced Western modes of production to the non-West and harmonized the world through technological breakthroughs in transportation and communications. As a result, most of the more than seven billion residents of the planet can now call practically any other instantaneously at reasonable costs, communicate electronically, or within twenty-four hours travel between any two major cities—as we witnessed in the case of Wuhan, China, ground zero of the Coronavirus epidemic.

But economic homogeneity and global connectedness soon led to the utopian idea of commensurate political uniformity. And here was the problem: while America spearheaded the global wealth creation, its unique constitutional system certainly did not become the model for political emulation. China has mimicked U.S. popular culture and elements of American free enterprise, but not our open society. During the epidemic, it lied about the origins, infectiousness, and lethality of the Coronavirus and shut down all travel to and from Wuhan, while it assured the world the threat was minimal and flights to the United States from Wuhan continued for days. In Europe, the French Revolution and the non-democratic autocracies and state bureaucracies that followed it became more of a blueprint for the European Union than the U.S. Bill of Rights and Declaration of Independence did. Poorer nations now look to richer Western systems that emphasize redistribution rather than those that emphasize equality of opportunity. Predictably, transnational institutions like the European Union, the United Nations and its affiliated commissions, the World Bank, the International Monetary Fund, and a host of others devoted to human rights, environmental protection, international commerce and trade, and health and welfare, became politicized. They insist on share-the-wealth policies and redistributive justice contrary to the U.S. Constitution, and, as we have seen in the case of the World Health Organization during the Coronavirus epidemic, are often critical of the United States, its major donor, in matters of life and death.

In the twenty-first century, America has begun to relearn that the laws of its Republic do not function on autopilot but must instead be carefully nourished and protected in the most practical of ways. The rise of the "cancel culture" of social media, an electronically charged "lynch mob" that can be activated in a nanosecond, means that both individuals and businesses deemed politically incorrect can be threatened with ostracism, boycotts, censure, and ruin.

For example, if rural citizens cannot find ammunition for their legal firearms due to ammunition-selling businesses' fear of censure, the Second Amendment can be rendered de facto irrelevant in places. In theory there is free speech on campuses; in fact, both students and professors accept that unpopular views voiced on issues such as abortion, affirmative action, or global warming can endanger grades and careers, respectively.

Given that federal prosecutors win or plea-bargain about 95 percent of their cases, any high-profile individual can be threatened with indictment and must then weigh the cost of a legal defense versus negotiation and avoidance of trial. Carter Page, a minor and temporary Trump campaign official in 2016, was surveilled by the U.S. government though the politicization and abuse of the FISA court warrant process, repeatedly interviewed and harassed by federal agents to leverage incriminating evidence against his employers, and yet never charged with a crime—a result that became apparent only after Page was forced to spend tens of thousands of dollars in preemptive legal fees. The so-called administrative state—whose investigators, auditors, and regulators are armed with unlimited legal resources and virtual lifetime job security but often lack much knowledge on how the private sector works—can all but ruin individuals and business concerns.

But postmodern citizenship is also more than a matter of adopting global norms in preference to U.S. customs and traditions, or using pressure groups to deny citizens their full protection of constitutional rights. There is currently a multitude of academic, legal, and political efforts to change either the U.S. Constitution or the custom and practice of the federal government. The common denominator in all these progressive and media agendas, both informal and legal, is the curbing of individual liberty and freedom as the necessary price to ensure an equality of result among all residents.

Furious that the current Supreme Court errs on the side of the individual rather than the collective interest? Then seek to resurrect something akin to Franklin Delano Roosevelt's shameful 1937 effort to pack the court by increasing the membership beyond the current nine justices. Or intimidate sitting justices with threats of mandatory retirement.

Upset that George W. Bush and Donald Trump both won elections without a majority of the national popular vote? Then seek either to disband the Electoral College or to pass state laws requiring a state to pledge its electors to the winner of the popular vote rather than to reflect the will of the majority of voters within a state.

Think it's unfair that the two conservative senators from Wyoming each represent roughly a quarter-million voters, while their liberal counterparts from California each speak for twenty million? Then seek to turn the U.S. Senate into something analogous to the House of Representatives, where congressional offices reflect national demography.

Believe that too many states vote conservatively? Then use the courts or the state legislatures to reduce the voting age to sixteen, abolish restrictions on voting rights for felons and ex-felons, and end requirements to show identification at the polls.

The list of proposed changes to both the Constitution and long legislative custom and practice that have been ratified and upheld by the courts is nearly endless. The effort is twofold. One aim is fundamentally to transform and recalibrate the American Republic to resemble a Jacobin sort of democracy in which whatever a majority of residents on any given day prefers becomes law.

The other aim is to institutionalize politically the vast cultural and economic changes that are turning the United States into a bi-coastal culture of rich and poor, with a forgotten and hollowed-out middle in between. That is, to bring into the electorate the sixteen-year-old, the illegal alien, and the felon in order to change the nature of the voter profile to counter the legal, law-abiding, and mature citizen, who is under suspicion of voting incorrectly—a sin often defined as merely being in accord with the Founders' visions of the Republic.

The result is that the United States is becoming a country of pre- and post-citizens. If we wonder why illegal alien residents who commit felonies are rarely deported or must be deported repeatedly, or why few college graduates know much about the Constitution and American history, or why loud social-justice-warrior athletes so eagerly mouth Chinese platitudes about curtailing free speech inside the United States, or why the protections offered by the First and Second Amendments depend largely on where you work or live, one of the reasons is because American citizenship as we once knew it is becoming meaningless.

The Idea of an American Nation

JAMES PIERESON

———◆———

Four score and seven years ago our fathers brought forth on this conti-
nent a new nation, conceived in liberty and dedicated to the proposition
that all men are created equal.
                                   —Abraham Lincoln, 1863

I BEGIN WITH a conclusion: the United States of America is near-
ing a point when it can no longer be described as a nation-state, in
the sense that term is generally used, and is evolving into a different
kind of enterprise—a multi-national, multi-cultural, multi-lingual,
and multi-ethnic state lacking the underpinnings of a common culture, language, religion, or nationality that we commonly associate
with modern nation-states.

This is due to several intersecting causes: destructive ideas (identity politics); large and apparently irresistible developments in the
world (globalism and large-scale migration); benign conditions that
erode national loyalties (peace and prosperity); and the unique character of the American nation (a nation-state built upon universal
principles). These have brought into being new lines of conflict in the
United States, with some rallying to preserve an inherited idea of the
American nation while others promote the forces that are eroding it.
Indeed, America's two political parties seem to be organizing themselves around this fundamental line of disagreement.

Many say that nationalism is a bad thing—that it is a cause of
wars, group hatreds, irrational conflicts, and the like—and that in the

interests of peace and harmony it should be discouraged or, better yet, eliminated altogether. This is an understandable point of view, in light of the violent national conflicts of all-too-recent memory. But if nationalism is bad, then so are nations and nation-states. Can we have nations without nationalism? Can we have an American nation absent some sense of American nationalism? Obviously not. It is all too easy to identify the vices of nationalism without appreciating its virtues. The United States, with its diversity of geography, conditions, and peoples, would have fallen apart long ago without the idea of a nation to hold it together. As a matter of history, nationalism was held out as the antidote to the tendency of the American union to split up and break apart. As the idea of an American nation retreats, the possibilities for break-up will advance at a similar rate.

Henry Adams wrote, somewhat in jest, that "Politics, whatever its professions, is the systematic organization of hatreds." That is not true, at least in regard to a successful politics, which depends upon a degree of comity and agreement—if only an agreement to disagree. A polity can function if people disagree with one another but not if they hate one another. People do not make mutual sacrifices on behalf of enemies. Pluralism is a good thing, up to a point, though it must rest upon an underlying agreement to abide by certain rules and to refrain from carrying things too far. The idea of a nation binds citizens into a common enterprise.

Yet today the United States seems headed in a different direction: toward pluralism without consensus, a nation-state without a national idea, and the "systematic organization of hatreds" among racial, religious, regional, and national groups. It is comforting to think that a "post-national" state will be a utopia of mutual tolerance and understanding. It could turn into something quite the opposite.

Will this new "post-national" state be able to function to resolve crises, address difficult issues, and deliver to Americans the kind of freedom and prosperity to which they have become accustomed as citizens of the world's most successful nation-state? Probably not. Is it still possible to restore the ideal of a single American nation? That remains to be seen.

David C. Hendrickson, in his admirable history of U.S. foreign relations titled *Union, Nation, or Empire* (2009), reminds us that the United States was not conceived in 1776 or 1787 as a nation-state but as a constitutional republic in the form of a union among states. The Founders thought in terms of both republicanism and union, though union proved to be the greater challenge because there existed a consensus at that time around the ideals of republicanism but not in regard to the foundation of a union among the states. Anti-Federalists claimed that a continental republic encompassing so many different states was a pipe dream. Advocates of the Constitution feared that without a stronger government the states might fly off on their own paths or form alliances with European powers. They—the Federalists—barely won the debate in 1787 and 1788 by persuading enough of their peers that the states and their inhabitants would find greater security and prosperity within the union than outside of it.

There was a widespread belief in the early years of the Republic that the Union, with its compromises between federal and state authority, represented a greater contribution to the cause of popular government than any other feature of the Constitution. Most federative systems, ancient and modern, had failed, usually because the parts spun off from the center, as Madison pointed out in making the case for union in *Federalist* Nos. 18, 19, and 20. The Constitution, and its formula for union, solved this perennial problem by granting the federal government sufficient powers to sustain itself while allowing state governments wide latitude to adjust to local conditions. Nevertheless, the original controversy between Federalists and Anti-Federalists recurred under different guises from 1789 to 1861, when the southern states finally seceded from the Union as others had threatened to do on several occasions in the intervening years. The Union, while an object of reverence, was at the same time continuously under threat of break-up, mainly due to the disparity of interests between the North and South.

At the time of the American founding, the empire (not the nation-state) was the established form of political organization over most of the civilized world. The Holy Roman Empire was still intact (barely), as were the Ottoman and the Russian Empires. Great Britain and France were well into the process of building overseas empires as attachments to fledgling nation-states. Empires ruled over large land areas, had fluid and unstable boundaries, and were composed of an array of ethnic, religious, and national groups co-existing within loose imperial federations. They were ruled dynastically by emperors, czars, and monarchs. The idea of a nation-state—a territorially large polity with fixed borders and a state representing a culturally distinct people—was yet to be developed as an alternative to empire. Though the term "nation" was in circulation at the time, it was mostly used as a synonym for "country."

For this reason, there was a marked tendency among members of the founding generation (Jefferson and Madison, principally) to conceive of the American union according to the imagery of empire. The United States, by virtue of the treaty with Great Britain that ended the revolution, acquired a vast expanse of territory west of the Appalachian Valley extending out to the Mississippi River. This brought about a far-reaching change in perspective among American leaders. The United States, up to that point a small coastal republic, now had control of territories that dwarfed European states in size and potential bounty.

Jefferson imagined an "empire of liberty," a boundless territory organized on the principles of republicanism that would stand as a bulwark against European empires looking for opportunities to expand in the Western hemisphere. He did not necessarily believe that the new republics had to organize themselves as offshoots of the American union but could co-exist as independent republics. Later, in 1820, he wrote that the sectional crisis could be resolved by allowing slavery to be "diffused" through the territories where it would no longer represent an overwhelming interest. That formula was rejected by the Missouri Compromise of that year, but resurrected in the 1850s, at which time it further inflamed sectional hostilities.

Jefferson's vision of an agrarian republic rested upon westward expansion, with political authority dispersed across a wide territory. Here was a key source of the dispute between Jefferson and Hamilton during the first decade under the Constitution. Hamilton envisioned a commercial republic, mostly coastal in nature and dependent upon commercial links with Great Britain, with an administrative center in the capital. Jefferson looked westward for the American future, Hamilton to the east, toward Europe, and especially toward Great Britain.

Madison, in making his case for the extended republic in *Federalist* 10, advanced a different but compatible theory—that by the application of representation and federalism (local self-government) there would be no territorial limits to the American union. Madison reconciled union, republicanism, and expansion within his theory of the extended republic. This was a rebuke to prominent theorists, Montesquieu and Rousseau specifically, who wrote that republics prospered only in small territorial units where citizens thought alike and held the same opinions. Here one might find the original seed of the modern nation-state. By contrast, Madison claimed that the multiplication of interests over a vast territory would be beneficial because such conflicts would cancel out one-another and forestall a concentration of power in the capital—thereby preserving the balance between the central government and the constituent states. It might be necessary occasionally and temporarily for these interests to unite in common cause, though mainly in response to threats from abroad. Otherwise, the self-cancelling conflicts held the system in equipoise, not unlike balance of power arrangements in the international system.

Some historians, Jacob Talmon, for example, in *The Rise of Totalitarian Democracy* (1952), have contrasted these theories with the nationalist ideas turned loose by the French Revolution. Madison wrote in *The Federalist* that, due to the operation of liberty, it would be impossible "to give to every citizen the same opinions, the same passions, and the same interests." Republican government had to accommodate—indeed, promote—a diversity of opinion and interests. The French revolutionaries thought differently. Jean-Paul Rabaut, one of the moderate leaders in the National Assembly in the early years of the Revolution (subsequently executed in the Terror), declared: "We must make the French a new people. We require an infallible means of transmitting constantly and immediately, to all the French at once, the same uniform ideas." Abbé Emmanuel Sieyès, another revolutionary theorist, wrote in a similar vein: "All parts of France must be made into a single body, and all the peoples who divide it into a single Nation. The national will needs only its reality to be always legal, it is the origin of all legality." Article three of *The Declaration of the Rights of Man and of the Citizen* asserts that, "The principle of all sovereignty resides essentially in the nation. No body nor individual may exercise any authority which does not proceed directly from the nation."

Revolutionary leaders sought to purify the French language, eliminate regional governments and loyalties, and construct a national religion as an alternative to Christianity. They thought a "nation" might be built on the model of the Catholic church, with a set of uniform beliefs, a catechism, and secular priests as leaders. The "nation" is "the people," everyone equal, united in a common outlook, and loyal to one another—and to the nation. "The nation," as Talmon wrote, "is not the aggregate of men, women and children but a confraternity of faith." This is the new language of nations and nation-building—a state linked to a culturally unified public. In contrast to the Americans of that time, the French theorists thought in terms of creating a nation—the first "new" nation built upon popular principles. They failed in this quest, or mostly failed, because a "nation" is a creation of time and events, and cannot be ordered into place at once.

It was Jefferson's vision of an "empire of liberty" that prevailed in the United States from 1800 to the southern secession in 1860–61. The American Union expanded its territory at an exponential rate in that period, thanks to Jefferson and his successors in the Democratic Party: Presidents Madison, Monroe, Jackson, and Polk. The United States doubled in size in 1803 by the Louisiana purchase, then expanded further with the annexation of Florida and later Texas, then added more territory in the southwest from the war with Mexico, and in the northwest (the Oregon territory) via negotiations with Great Britain. The United States was by 1850 an ocean-bound republic with no obvious end in sight to further expansion. President Polk, in his inaugural address in 1845, declared that, "It is confidently believed that our system may be safely extended to the utmost bounds of our territorial limits, and that as it shall be extended the bonds of our Union…will become stronger." He was wrong with regard to the "bonds of union," which were coming apart due to anxieties over expansion. Some in the South at that time began to look to the Caribbean islands as means of extending a slave empire; some in the North, looking to balance such extensions, thought about the acquisition of Canada, or parts of it.

No one today looking at a map of the United States as of 1850 would conclude that it resembled a modern nation-state. The country's borders continually expanded over a fifty-year period due to land purchases, conquest, annexations, and treaties with European empires. The country was equally divided between free and slave states, with new occasions for sectional conflict arising every year, and each side looking for ways to break the stalemate. Those living in North and South formed loyalties to their respective sections. People from other countries entered the United States freely and with little overall regulation because the federal government had yet to seize control of immigration policy from the individual states. The vast interior of the country, running from the Mississippi River to the Pacific Ocean, was mostly open land, and yet to be settled and organized. Hostile native tribes controlled large swaths of it and were poised to resist further incursions into their territories. Under such circumstances, the "bonds of union" inevitably frayed.

This was an exceptional polity due to its scale, its popular foundations, its rapid growth, absence of inherited ranks, and so much more. But what was it: union, republic, or empire—or a combination of all three? Whatever it was, it was not yet a nation.

. . .

The United States forged itself into a nation—into a nation-state—over a ninety-year period from 1860 to 1950, an era book-ended by the Civil War and World War II, two great wars for liberal democracy, with World War I sandwiched in between. These were communal events: all Americans participated in one way or another. They called for widespread sacrifice: many thousands were killed, and many more thousands wounded, in conflicts of unprecedented scale. These wars, tragic though they were, assimilated millions of immigrants into the national culture, and they provided momentum for the post-war civil rights movement that sought to integrate African-Americans into the nation. If you or your son or daughter or your husband or close relative fought for America, then no one could say you were not an American. The experience of war-bound Americans into a common national enterprise, creating over the decades an ever more coherent image of an American "people" represented by a national state. If in 1860 the United States was a hybrid of different polities, then by 1950 there is little doubt that it had transformed itself into a modern nation.

It was Abraham Lincoln who first conceived the idea of an American nation as a solution to the sectional warfare that eventually broke apart the Union. Lincoln began to use the term "nation" as an alternative to "union" early in his career when he saw sectional divisions escalating at the same time as the revolutionary generation had passed away—Madison, the last of the living Founders, died in 1836. With the Founders gone and memories of the Revolution fading away, what would hold the Union together and bind its people to a common enterprise?

Lincoln envisioned a nation held together by a "political religion" based upon reverence for the Founding Fathers, the Constitution, and the Declaration of Independence. During the sectional crisis of the 1850s, he held up the Declaration as "the sheet anchor of American republicanism," and invoked the Founding Fathers in the campaign to place limits on the expansion of slavery. In his Gettysburg Address, delivered in the midst of war when the outcome was yet in doubt, he expressed the idea of the nation in semi-religious terms: "Four score and seven years ago our fathers brought forth on this continent a new nation, conceived in liberty and dedicated to the proposition that all men are created equal." This was not technically true, since the idea of a nation was yet to be developed in 1776; nonetheless, it was necessary to buttress the idea of a nation by linking it to the hopes of the Founding Fathers. The Civil War, mixed with Lincoln's leadership and sublime rhetoric, established the idea of an indivisible American nation as anchored in the Declaration and Constitution. Among his achievements, this must be counted among the most significant: conceiving and beginning the transition of the United States from union to nation.

This did not happen all at once, since even as Lincoln was speaking at Gettysburg half of the nation was still at war with the other half, and a good portion of northern opinion was sympathetic to the South and hostile to Lincoln. He was responsible for the idea of the American nation, though perhaps not for the reality of it. That would be the work of time and events: the development of railroads, highways, and means of communication that cemented the American people and the states into a coherent nation with secure and stable borders, along with the wars and conflicts of the first half of the twentieth century that bound Americans together by mutual sacrifices. The American welfare state, expressed in the New Deal and the Great Society, could not have been built absent the development of a national community to sustain the idea that "we are all in this together." It is easy to take the nation for

19

no longer

granted today, but it was the work of a century, requiring enormous effort and sacrifice, that transformed the United States from a hopelessly divided union into the world's most powerful nation-state.

Because of the central role of the Declaration of Independence in validating the Revolution, and Lincoln's success in establishing it as the central symbol of American nationality, it is logical to conclude that the United States is a "proposition" nation founded on a commitment to abstract principles (rather than loyalty to cultural, ethnic, or national groups). It is, in Hans Kohn's terminology, a "civic" nation based upon a civic creed emphasizing liberty and democracy rather than an "ethnic" nation based upon cultural or ethnic loyalties. The United States is held together by loyalty to political institutions and abstract ideals—as in Lincoln's "political religion."

This, while largely so, admits of considerable qualification. Beginning in the founding era, Americans were aware that their country had important cultural underpinnings: it was British, English speaking, and Protestant. Those categories were enlarged during the nineteenth century to include Catholics and non-English speaking Europeans (mostly Germans). There was a racial element, of which everyone was aware. The first Naturalization Act (1790) limited citizenship to members of the white race, an act that was repealed after the Civil War by the Fourteenth Amendment. In 1882, Congress passed the Chinese Exclusion Act prohibiting the immigration of Chinese laborers (the entrance of Chinese women had been banned some years earlier), a law that was on the books until 1943 and not fully repealed until 1965. The Immigration Act of 1924, enacted on a bipartisan basis, barred all immigration from Asia and set national quotas favoring immigration from Canada and northern Europe. President Coolidge said when he signed the bill that, "We cast no aspersions on any race or creed, but we must remember that every object of our institutions of society and Government will fail unless America be kept American." As late as 1942 President Roosevelt could say, "The United States is a Protestant country and Catholics are here at their sufferance." The idea of an

American nation, shaped so much by Lincoln's political religion, also had an unmistakable cultural dimension.

Over the course of the post-war era, the foundations of that American nation—the cultural nation—have gradually washed away, but without being replaced by new ones to keep the national enterprise together. The Immigration Act of 1965, which repealed the national origins quotas in the 1924 act, opened the country to immigrants from Asia, Africa, and Latin America in numbers never anticipated by the authors of the 1965 legislation. As a result, the United States is now home to an endless variety of linguistic, religious, and cultural groups. The Protestant, or European, or English-speaking nation is giving way to a multicultural, multilingual, and multinational country in which differences between the new and old groups are celebrated and reinforced. It is no longer possible for the United States to go forward as a "cultural" nation in the form by which it developed between 1860 and 1950. Whether or not this is a good thing is beside the point: it has happened, is happening, and will continue to happen.

As the cultural nation recedes, the United States could go forward as a "civic" nation, on the basis of Lincoln's "political religion" or loyalty to the nation's political institutions. In the history of nations, a purely "civic" nation would be something new. The United States, an exceptional nation, might be the first of that kind. Yet the nation's political ideals, and their associated institutions, have also come under sustained attack by many who also celebrate the nation's growing cultural diversity. They loudly assert that the Founding Fathers were slave owners and therefore hypocrites; the Declaration of Independence is a fraud; the Constitution favors the rich and stands in the way of needed change; Lincoln was a white supremacist; the American past is a tale of oppression, conquest, and environmental degradation. Such views are circulated in America's schools, colleges, textbooks, and board rooms, and they are popular among journalists, professors, and political activists. Through these attacks, the "civic" nation is disappearing almost as rapidly as the "cultural" nation.

These developments leave the United States without any strong foundation to keep itself together as a political enterprise—in a circumstance when its increasing diversity requires some kind of unifying thread. At one time the idea of Union held the enterprise together, then later the idea of an American nation. What would that new thread look like, and how would it weave together the disparate groups making up the American polity? No one now knows. But unless it is somehow found, the United States is at risk of blowing itself apart in the twenty-first century, as it did once before in the middle of the nineteenth.

Sovereignty & Its Enemies

JOHN FONTE

———◆———

I N MY BOOK *Sovereignty or Submission* (Encounter, 2011), I argued
that we needed to reconfigure the global chess board of world
politics. The sovereign democratic nation-state faces two adversaries,
one hard and one soft: authoritarian regimes such as China, Russia,
and Iran; and also the oligarchical forces of global governance ema-
nating from within the democratic world itself.

Transnational progressives, or globalists, represent a major
challenge to democratic nation-states because they seek to transfer
political decision-making from democratic nations to supranational authorities and institutions. The decades-long trajectory of the
European Union is an example of this phenomenon.

These globalists include the leadership of the United Nations
and the European Union; bureaucrats from the World Trade Organization and the International Monetary Fund; judges from the
European Court of Human Rights and the International Criminal Court; career officials in the U.S. State Department, the British Foreign Office, and the German Foreign Ministry; American CEOs of major global corporations; employees of NGOs such
as Amnesty International, Human Rights Watch, and Greenpeace;
and prominent American international relations specialists and
international lawyers, including the leadership of the American
Bar Association.

But another anti-sovereignty force is simultaneously at work:
the American democracy promotion network. What role, if any,

do the promoters of democracy play in the worldwide ideological conflict between democratic sovereigntists and globalists?

The American democracy promotion network is based in organizations such as the National Endowment for Democracy (NED) and Freedom House and includes an array of prominent writers. Created by the U.S. Congress in 1983 to "strengthen democratic values and institutions around the world through nongovernmental efforts," the NED is a tax-exempt, non-profit private corporation. It is funded annually by Congress and achieved prominence during the Cold War. Freedom House was founded in 1941 by Wendell Willkie and Eleanor Roosevelt to be a "clear voice for freedom and democracy around the world." After the Cold War, its private funding dried up. Freedom House is now almost entirely dependent on the federal government. For years, both NED and Freedom House have been considered non-partisan. But the world has changed.

A major front in this worldwide conflict has been the struggle over Brexit. On August 28, 2019 NED's daily online journal, the *Democracy Digest*, declared, "Nakedly Populist move jolts world's most stable democracy." It linked to an article by liberal Harvard professor Yascha Mounk stating that Boris Johnson's decision to suspend Parliament temporarily is "the most blatant assault on democracy in Britain's living memory." Mounk (a major contributor to NED journals) continued, "the big question I've heard asked about Boris Johnson is whether it's right to characterize him as an authoritarian populist in the mold of America's Donald Trump or Italy's Matteo Salvini."

A week later, on September 4, 2019, *Democracy Digest* linked to an essay by Ian Buruma asserting that "Boris Johnson poses the same dangers to liberal democracy that populist agitators did to the Roman Republic." In fact, for months before the Tory election victory in December 2019 the NED journal continuously linked to anti-Brexit articles day in and day out. They rarely, if ever, linked to Brexit supporters such as Daniel Hannan or Douglas Murray.

Freedom House also disparages the Brexiteers. Its influential annual report in 2018 stated that the Brexit campaign "brought widespread concerns of rising anti-immigrant and anti-Muslim sentiment in the country with the Council of Europe expressing concerns about hate speech among politicians and in popular tabloid newspapers." Is Freedom House implying that political speech should be restricted?

It's not just Brexit that has been a focus for these institutions. For the past several years, the democratically elected conservative governments in Poland and Hungary have been under continuous assault from the NED, Freedom House, and the global governance movement generally. They are accused of so-called "democratic backsliding."

For instance, the NED's print magazine, the *Journal of Democracy*, in October 2016 published a special section on "The Specter Haunting Europe." Eight pro-EU authors attributed the success of patriotic, culturally and religiously conservative democratic political parties to the dark forces of "authoritarianism," "democratic regression," and "populism" (which always has a negative connotation). Typical was an essay declaring that "the 2015 victory of Poland's Law and Justice Party is an example of the rise of contemporary authoritarian populism."

Another special section in the *Journal of Democracy* of July 2018, "Explaining Eastern Europe," argued that "populist" (as opposed to democratic sovereigntist) electoral success relied on "the willingness of politicians to use fear and anxiety," most often about "mass migration and terrorism." NED authors tell us that "nativist parties that thrive on fears regarding immigration and continuing European integration" must be "contain[ed]."

In other words, NED essayists are saying that democratic nation-states that oppose further EU integration and that wish to determine their own immigration policy are somehow "undemocratic" and thus require lessons on "democratic values" from a political entity (the European Union) in which laws are initiated by an unelected bureaucracy rather than by an elected legislature.

Poland and Hungary are often charged with undermining an independent judiciary—the rule of law. In both countries since the fall of communism, judiciaries were self-perpetuating oligarchies with little input from elected officials. New judges were chosen by sitting judges and committees of lawyers, leading to widespread nepotism and corruption. Imagine if in the United States federal judges were chosen by the American Bar Association, or if judges on the Ninth Circuit chose their own successors. This is not "the rule of law," but the rule of lawyers.

In fact, the conservative governments in Poland and Hungary are essentially reforming their judiciaries, making them more in line with democracies like the United States, in which democratically elected officials are part of the process of choosing judges.

Poland and Hungary are not, however, the only conservative governments that are seen as problematic. Freedom House downgraded Israel's civil liberties rating in 2018 because the conservative Likud government passed the NGO Transparency Law. The law required non-profit organizations that received more than half their funding from foreign sources (mostly from the European Union and individual European states) to disclose this information. Prime Minister Netanyahu stated that "the purpose of the law is to prevent the absurd situation in which foreign countries intervene in Israel's internal affairs without the Israeli public even being aware of it." For Freedom House, the law constitutes "intolerance of dissent."

In the same annual report, Freedom House declared that Denmark's right-of-center government deserved "special scrutiny" because its parliament considered legislation that would "restrict immigrant rights." Specifically, the Danish government reduced cash welfare benefits for refugees and required affluent migrants to pay for their own support rather than use government welfare funds. For Freedom House, this apparently constitutes "setbacks for freedom."

Is there a pattern here? The "illiberals," "populists," and "nativists" always represent conservative democratic sovereigntist political forces (usually friendly, one might add, to traditional Christianity and Judaism), whether in Great Britain, Poland, Hungary, Israel, or Denmark. And, of course, in the United States.

In 2014, before there was a President Trump, Freedom House condemned voter identification laws as Republican attempts to suppress minority voting. Since Trump's election, we have seen the emergence of a grand narrative of a rising illiberalism in the West, which is allegedly now aligned with authoritarianism. The narrative runs along these lines: Putin equals Erdoğan equals Orbán equals Kaczyński equals Netanyahu equals Brexit equals Trump. As one NED essay put it, "Europe" [i.e., the European Union] faces "Islamism to the south, Putin to the east, Brexit and Trump to the west."

But it's not just Europe that's purportedly entering a parlous state. In 2019, Michael Abramowitz, President of Freedom House, declared that "the pillars of freedom have come under attack here in the United States." He cited the Trump administration's "harsh attack on immigrants [*n.b.* failing to distinguish between illegal and legal immigrants] and asylum seekers [that] have restricted their rights." And what would those rights be? Apparently, the right of any person to enter a democracy without the consent of the citizens of that democracy.

Larry Diamond of Stanford is the co-editor of the NED's *Journal of Democracy*. He has studied democratic development around the world for decades. Diamond told *The New York Times* that the Trump administration poses a worse threat to democracy than Watergate and that "Hillary Clinton would almost certainly have won" the presidency if not for Russian interference.

Robert Kagan of the Brookings Institution is a close associate of the democracy promotion network. His wife Victoria Nuland (who was a key player in the Obama State Department under Hillary Clinton) has served on the board of the NED. On the issue of sovereignty, Kagan declared in 2008 that the "United States…should not oppose, but welcome, a world of pooled and diminished national sovereignty."

"Democracy embattled"

In January 2020 the *Journal of Democracy* published its thirtieth-anniversary issue. Co-editor Marc Plattner explained that the phrase

"Democracy Embattled" reflected the mood among the leadership at the NED and its allies. Plattner wrote that today, both domestically and internationally, "Democracy is under assault." In his introductory essay Plattner identifies *external* and *internal* threats to democracy. Not surprisingly, he cites China, Russia, and Iran as external opponents to the democratic world. True enough.

However, in examining the "internal" challenge the situation becomes murkier. Plattner tells us that "a sudden shift has taken place in the so-called advanced democracies, mostly belonging to the West." The "deep-rootedness and stability of these regimes" can no longer be "taken for granted." The challenge comes from "populism," however this phenomenon is understood.

Also in the thirtieth anniversary issue, Francis Fukuyama, more directly, decries the democratic "backsliding that has lately occurred in the most consolidated democracies (including the United States and Britain)." He declares that "Brexit has fractured the British political system" and "Donald Trump has challenged many of America's check and balance institutions." But, he remarks, don't worry because "Over the long run, demographics do not seem to favor populism; young people continue to move out of rural areas and into big cities."

Yascha Mounk writes in the same vein as Fukuyama, while being even more explicit. Mounk laments that "populist forces intent on challenging the most basic rules and norms of liberal democracy have risen across a great swath of democratic countries." Indeed, Mounk describes, "An onslaught of bad news; from the election of Donald Trump to the death throes of democracies in Hungary and Venezuela."

For Mounk the "tides of history are rapidly turning....Over the span of less than a decade, Great Britain voted for Brexit, the United States elected Donald Trump, authoritarian populists took the reins of power from Brazil to India and from Italy to the Philippines, and elected strongmen started an all-out assault on liberal democracy in Ankara, Budapest, Caracas, Moscow, and Warsaw."

Professor Mounk is engaging in a crude, dishonest smear campaign

(what Harvard progressives once called "McCarthyism"). He is con-
flating conservative democratic politicians, Republicans in the United
States, and Tory Brexiteers in the United Kingdom with Russian and
Venezuelan authoritarians. Likewise, there is no legitimate comparison between an open, democratic politician like Italy's Salvini with the
thuggish Duterte in the Philippines. The comparisons between Hungary and Venezuela and between Warsaw and Moscow are outrageous.

Unlike the coercive regime in Venezuela, there is no Cuban secret
police-militant paramilitary apparatus in Hungary that represses political opponents. On the contrary, opponents of the elected government
operate as freely in Hungary as they do in any Western European democracy. There is plenty of media criticism of Prime Minister Orbán
and the opposition recently won an electoral victory in the capital of
Budapest in a free and fair election.

The leading political party in Poland (Law and Justice) is a conservative, democratic, traditionalist, Roman Catholic–oriented political
party. As in Hungary, the political opposition operates freely, recently
won an election in the nation's capital, and vigorously and openly op-
poses the government in the media. And, also, as in Hungary (and, for
that matter, in the United States and most democratic countries) Poland
prefers to implement its own immigration policy rather than outsourc-
ing this essential exercise of national sovereignty to foreign bodies.

True, the Law and Justice leadership and political supporters throughout the country are mostly practicing Catholics. Therefore, they support
the traditional family, oppose abortion, and are not interested in banishing
religion from the public square. No doubt, this retrograde outlook irritates
progressive bien-pensant thinking from Warsaw to Washington D.C., but
this does not make conservative, democratic Poland a twin of Putin's authoritarian regime that ultimately relies on intimidation and force.

So what is going on?

At the very least, the NED is not adhering to its congressionally mandated mission of strengthening democratic values in a non-partisan

manner. Neither is Freedom House faithful to its strategic vision of being a clear voice for freedom and democracy around the world. To be sure, there is a difference between the work of these two organizations in places beset by genuine authoritarian regimes such as Venezuela, Cuba, China, Iran, and North Korea—work that is sometimes commendable—and their partisan activities in North America and Europe.

Clearly, in the West, the NED, Freedom House, and their stable of writers are highly partisan, anti-conservative, anti-sovereignty, militantly secular, and more supportive of oligarchical elites than democratic majorities. They single out for criticism Denmark's immigration policy, Israel's transparency approach to foreign-funded NGOs, and Poland's restrictions on abortion, because they are allied with transnational progressives on crucial democratic and social issues.

When examining Brexit, the European Union, or mass migration in Europe and the United States, the democracy promoters quote and link to *The Guardian*, George Soros's Open Society Foundation, Yascha Mounk, Fareed Zakaria, Francis Fukuyama, and Robert Kagan, not to *The Telegraph*, Roger Scruton, Christopher Caldwell, or John O'Sullivan. In sum, they are not balanced. This should be of particular interest since their core organizations (the NED and Freedom House) are overwhelmingly subsidized by American taxpayers on the false assumption that they are non-partisan.

Further, there little or no criticism of the European Union's long-recognized "democracy deficit" along the lines of the former German Foreign Minister Joschka Fischer's famous Humboldt University speech in May of 2000. Generally, there is there no criticism of the European Union's blatant illiberalism. (By illiberalism I mean, for instance, gender and ethnic quotas, and highly restrictive hate speech measures which distort the debate in the public square on issues related to mass migration, immigrant criminality, and radical Islamic terrorism.)

There is no criticism of Angela Merkel for pressuring Mark Zuckerberg to censor online denunciation of her immigration policies. Indeed, German illiberalism surpasses anything going on in Poland or Hungary, where (as noted) the opposition recently carried Warsaw and Budapest in free elections. Why does the United States rate lower than Germany in Freedom House's rankings?

Marc Plattner, the co-editor of the *Journal of Democracy*, asked whether American conservatives are giving up on liberal democracy. The answer is of course not. Conservatives are embracing democratic sovereignty and rejecting undemocratic transnational governance. They are saying that President Donald Trump was right to tell the United Nations that "Sovereign and independent nations are the only vehicle where freedom has ever survived, and democracy ever endured."

Plattner himself, in his book *Democracy Without Borders?*, conceded that the European Union had a "democracy deficit," while at the same time writing (somewhat ambiguously), "I am not arguing that European unification as such is hostile to democracy, or that the only way to preserve democracy in Europe is to reaffirm the sovereignty of the EU's member states. I am not a 'Euroskeptic.'" But, of course, reaffirming the national sovereignty of democratic nation-states is the only way to preserve democracy in Europe or, for that matter, anywhere else in the world.

The challenges to democracy from the administrative state and an activist judiciary are ignored

Serious students of democracy have long examined the problems that an overweening bureaucracy and a politically activist judiciary pose to elected self-government. For example, the Claremont Institute's John Marini for decades has immersed himself in the intricacies of the administrative state, an unaccountable bureaucracy that in the United States has to a large extent usurped much of the power of the elected branches of government (the Congress and the Presidency) and, thereby, upset the constitutional balance of power.

Marini writes that in the United States, "the [administrative state] bureaucracy, and the political, economic, and social forces beholding

31

to it, have sought to progressively replace politics by substituting administrative rulemaking for general lawmaking and to rule by expert in place of that by elected official."

I suggest that in the European Union, the European Commission acts as a type of administrative state. It is an unelected administrative body that also has the power to initiate legislation. The modern administrative state, whether in North America or Europe, is the twenty-first-century bureaucratic challenge to democracy foreseen by nineteenth- and early-twentieth-century thinkers including Tocqueville, Weber, Michels, Pareto, and Mosca. Unfortunately, these rich analyses of the problematic crossroads between unelected bureaucracy and political democracy (or government by consent of the governed) do not seem to have greatly piqued the interest of the American theoreticians of democracy promotion allied to the NED and Freedom House.

In 2003, the late Judge Robert Bork wrote (in *Coercing Virtue: Worldwide Rule of Judges*) that judiciaries throughout the West were overreaching and acting as legislators, by making laws rather than interpreting statutes created by elected representatives of the people. Judge Bork labeled this judicial activism or "judicial imperialism."

He writes: "Judicial imperialism is manifest everywhere.... We have seen activism at work in the United States, Canada, Israel, Europe, and tribunals claiming worldwide jurisdiction." The main problem, Bork tells us, is that "the rule of law has become confused with—indeed subverted by—the rule of judges. That subversion is exactly what judicial activism accomplishes. . . . Activism elevates the objectives of a dominant minority above the democratic process."

Why have so many judges in the West become activists who usurp the authority of elected officials? Because, Bork suggests, many judges are ideologically committed to a progressive worldview which is anti-majoritarian. In other words, these judges are not in favor of traditional limited government, but in fact, are in favor of an even larger government albeit, under minority (or oligarchical) rather than majority or democratic rule.

Thus, seventeen years ago, Bork wrote "In reading the opinions of many judges, it is apparent that they view their mission as preserving civilization from a barbarian majority motivated by bigotry, racism, sexism, xenophobia, irrational sexual morality, and the like."

In sum, many scholars, analysts, and politicians from democratic nations see unresponsive bureaucracies and imperial judiciaries rather than "populism" or "nativism" as the paramount challenges to democratic self-government. Committing a major sin of omission, this entire body of historical and contemporary argument has not been seriously examined, or even acknowledged, by the NED's *Journal of Democracy*, *Democracy Digest*, or Freedom House reports.

Conclusion

In this essay I have focused on the American democracy promotion network because in a practical, operational sense, this network is a key asset for the global progressives in their campaign against democratic sovereignty.

The democracy promotion network continues to be influential because it retains support among Republicans in Congress and in the foreign policy establishment. Old habits die hard. Many Republican politicians think we are still living in Francis Fukuyama's dreamworld in which there is a unified democratic West, instead of today's reality—a world playing host to a global struggle between democratic sovereignty and transnational progressivism.

The democracy promotion network needs to be called out and demystified. At the very least, these actors are not doing what they are being paid to do with taxpayer dollars.

In the thirtieth anniversary issue of the *Journal of Democracy*, co-editor Plattner noted (correctly) that "the demand for democracy is still remarkably robust." He quoted NED President Carl Gerschman's comment that the "instinct for freedom remains strong."

True, indeed. But, ironically, the democracy promoters at the NED, Freedom House, and their allies in the media and on Capitol

Hill fail to recognize this instinct for freedom (for democratic self-government) when it comes from the majority of the British people in the form of Brexit, and when it reflects the conservative, traditionalist, religious, and patriotic aspirations of ordinary citizens and political forces throughout Central and Western Europe, the Americas, and the rest of the world.

The Left v. the Nation

JOHN O'SULLIVAN

◆

I T SOMETIMES seems to me, and perhaps to you if you have read me frequently, that I have been talking and writing about American nationalism ever since I arrived in America as an immigrant in 1979. In fact, my epiphany came somewhat later. It was not until the special issue of *National Review* devoted to "Demystifying Multiculturalism" in February 1994 that I came out of the closet as a "nationalist for America." That seems a better description of my standpoint than "American nationalist," since I was then and have remained since a loyal subject of Queen Elizabeth II. The impulse to engage with such issues as multiculturalism and immigration came not from a personal transfer of patriotic loyalty from Britain to America—much though I love and admire the latter—but rather from the intellectual conviction that the dominant multiculturalist doctrine of American nationality was a simple error that, if persisted in, would have disastrous results.

Nationalism has many definitions, but the one employed here is the concept that people come to share a national identity, mutual loyalty, and sense of fellowship and common destiny as the result of sharing the same language and culture and of living under the same institutions over a long period of time. A nation may have many different historical origins—dynastic, ethnic, revolutionary, etc. What matters is that over time its people come to feel that they are part of the same collective body and feel a loyalty to it and its symbols, whether the monarchy in the United Kingdom or the flag in the United States. Their attachment to the nation comes less from its theoretical virtue than from the experience of living contentedly in a society that reflects one's own tastes and gives opportunities to realize oneself. A national identity of this kind is taken for granted rather than self-consciously chosen.

All that seemed commonsense to me. The doctrine of nationalism that I thought mistaken was the one based on the "American Creed." This defined Americans as a "creedal nation" unlike any other: a people who were united neither by ethnicity nor by loyalty to a dynastic sovereign but instead by a set of liberal principles, principally liberty and equality. That struck me not as false—in fact it contained important truths about America—so much as inadequate. The liberty that Americans prized, for instance, was a political idea usually associated with the English political philosopher John Locke that was brought to America by the English colonists. Liberty comes in at the beginning of the American story. But as Paul Johnson celebrated in his enthusiastic *History of the American People* (1997), this liberty flowered to its full potential in the geographic and economic space of the New World.

America's bigness was a political and philosophical fact of the first importance, and it made liberty a different thing. It meant that land was cheap, labor expensive, and government distant to the degree that a man might earn a family farm by his labor in a few years. To a people who enjoyed this independence either in practice or in possibility, Locke's philosophy seemed simple commonsense.

The principles of the Declaration of Independence sustained in the Creed were a philosophical distillation of the lived freedom that the American colonists had created, the American rebels had made a universal possibility, and that millions of immigrants subsequently embraced with gratitude and made their own. All of them would happily recite America's sacred documents such as the Gettysburg Address and sing its popular songs such as "Yankee Doodle Dandy" on the Fourth of July. But it was the common culture of lived freedom that underpinned those ceremonies and that united the American people. Over time and through better communications this common culture encompassed more and more aspects of life and helped shape more and more people.

My favorite illustration of this comes from the Second World War, by which time all but the most recent migrants had become culturally American. When German commandos disguised in U.S. uniforms were conducting sabotage and murder behind American lines during the Battle of the Bulge, the G.I.s testing the identity of potential SS men asked not about anarchism or the First Amendment but questions designed to expose their knowledge (or ignorance) of everyday American life. That produced some unexpected effects. General Marshall corrected his American inquisitor's claim that the capital of Illinois was Chicago; Britain's Field Marshal Montgomery imperiously waved aside the U.S. guards, who promptly shot out his tires; and the actor David Niven (then a British commando), on being asked by the Americans who had won the 1943 World Series, replied: "Haven't the foggiest idea, but I did co-star with Ginger Rogers in *Bachelor Mother.*"

If my argument is right here, the American Creed is inadequate as a definition of a People. Its ideas are not as distinctive as the culture in which they're embedded, even when that culture has been transmitted to the world by Hollywood, television, and the internet. Liberal ideas found in the American Creed were and are shared by liberally minded people all over the world—most fervently in other English-speaking countries which had inherited the same ideas even if they sometimes interpreted them differently, but elsewhere too. As the United States rose to international power, these liberals looked to it as a sort of savior. That is the practical meaning of America as mankind's last best hope. But it does not mean that everyone alive wants to be an American or is already a proto-American rather than what he is. Liberal-minded people in other lands usually want their own version of a liberal constitution and a free society.

As daily becomes more apparent, a creedal nationality gradually becomes a vehicle for multiculturalism, which is itself, as the late Samuel Huntington argued in *Who Are We?* (his final and most important book from 2004), a recipe for "the deconstruction of America." If America is essentially the embodiment of liberal political ideas, why should the language, culture, and institutions of the original settlers enjoy preference in law and custom over those same attributes and interests of the newer migrants? Provided that the bearers of these new cultures are prepared to eliminate, put in cold storage, or deny their more illiberal features, these immigrants have as much "right" to see their beliefs reflected in the common culture in American political and legal institutions as the founding generations. Properly speaking, there is no "American culture" in this constitutional vision, rather many American cultures. Thus the creedal nation becomes over time a multicultural patchwork quilt.

This is a vision of nationality that is likely to appeal to lawyers, bureaucrats, academics, and intellectuals far more than to ordinary citizens. For starters, it will provide them with almost continuous well-paid employment, interpreting old rules in line with new rights and settling disputes between different ethno-cultural groups. It also replaces the comforting solidarity that a national idea should provide ordinarily with a constant ethnic and interest-group conflict. Or, as Al Gore correctly understood but incorrectly translated *E Pluribus Unum*: "Out of One, Many."

Despite these drawbacks, it seemed to me twenty-five years ago that support for the creedal theory was bipartisan. Conservative intellectuals—especially but not only neo-conservatives—were as strongly attached to it, as were intellectuals of the Left. My antipathy towards the idea of a creedal nation was probably excessive then, but all the same the situation has changed dramatically. Since the 2016 primary season, Americans have been talking about nationalism all the time. That is because, as Huntington predicted and as James Piereson argues in this volume, the American nation is under serious threat of dissolution. One of the two main parties now supports policies of de facto open borders, mass immigration, accelerated multiculturalism, and the elimination of policies that distinguish between citizens and non-citizens. The second reason is that Donald Trump took up the cause of the nation in 2016 when almost all other Republican candidates resolutely refused to do so. Mr. Trump would not be my chosen poster boy for American nationalism, in part because he does not articulate the national question in depth. But he took up the task. Others must now develop the arguments for it—and, alas, they probably have to be intellectuals.

Some conservative intellectuals have already stepped up to the plate. Yoram Hazony, Rich Lowry, and Michael Anton have all produced books defending nationalism against its more hysterical critics. Magazines like the *Claremont Review of Books* and *American Affairs* have arisen to expose the Left's more romantic justifications for multiculturalism and mass migration to skeptical enquiry. And some magazines, *The New Criterion* and *National Review* for instance, never abandoned such criticisms. To be sure, there are still conservative intellectuals committed to the creedal version of American identity, and they don't lack reasons. In a society that has already received millions of recent immigrants, both conservative sides can agree on the need to promote a greater sense of community across different ethno-cultural groups even if we differ on how to do so. These immigrants, when all is said and done, are all Americans or likely to be. And we should want to strengthen the ties of national solidarity uniting us all.

That is not equally true of the Left, which, as we shall see, is ambivalent about national solidarity if it conflicts with human equality and policies of global redistribution. By the Left I mean a variety of political and philosophical groups which define themselves as opposed in principle to the existing order of society and hopeful of constructing a better one.

My definition does not include groups of urban or agricultural workers who protest against manifest social evils or organize in order to improve their living standards. Marx's proletariat was never really a sovereign actor of the Left, nor was it meant to be by socialists. It was a horse whose rider was the vanguard of intellectuals who understood where history was going. As history proceeded, largely disproving the theories of the vanguard, the proletariat emancipated itself from the control of the Left and adopted its own priorities that were rooted in collective democratic self-help, a common culture shaped by Christian values, and—since the world was organized along nation-state lines—a decent, respectable, and largely pacific patriotism. In short, the proletariat proved a great disappointment to the early Marxists because it declared itself to be part of the nation. In 1867 Engels wrote to Marx following Disraeli's victory in that year's election: "Once again the English working class has disgraced itself."

It's hardly surprising therefore that the Left has been either hostile or ambivalent to the idea of the nation. If we look at the fifty-seven varieties of Leftism, we find that each one treats the nation as an obstacle to the realization of its aims.

Marxist socialists see the nation as an undesirable alternative to what should be the worker's true focus of loyalty, namely his class. Both Marx and Lenin conceded that national liberation movements could play a limited part in hastening the demise of feudalism, capitalism, imperialism, etc. But they recognized and distrusted the power of such movements. And once in power themselves, they cautiously embraced an apolitical form of cultural nationalism to appease the subjects of the Soviet empire. As Anthony Daniels has written of the folkloric displays seen by every foreign delegation to Moscow: "Under communism all minorities dance." It didn't work; nationalism was one of the forces that brought communism down.

Progressives similarly see an effective self-governing nation as an obstacle to their system of elite rule by experts. They don't believe that democratically elected politicians should be able to override decisions reached "scientifically" by trained minds. A Tocquevillian nation engenders special hostility among progressives as it disperses social decisions down to the lowest possible level, rendering elites even less necessary than in a centralized democracy. This progressive hostility to democracy has been surprisingly candid and strong in the reaction against Brexit in both Europe and America, where elite institutions like the media, though knowing little about it, instantly recognized the referendum as a threat to . . . well, something or other.

Postmodernists in the mold of Michel Foucault or, worse, critical race or legal theorists, see the national idea as a mask of power wielded by the elites they wish to replace, since it mobilizes popular support for the status quo and particular policies. Experience suggests the opposite: it is they who wield the relevant power, and critical race theory is a mask of their power. As Andrew Sullivan pointed out in his important article on the 1619 Project of *The New York Times*, when the American paper of record presents a view of the United States derived almost entirely from critical race theory as a simple compendium of historical facts, it is absurd to claim that a white-supremacist establishment is calling the shots everywhere. This particular Left has made a fetish of its impotence so as to attain absolute power in universities, the media, and publishing. It now wields it all but absolutely. But popular democratic sovereignty in a national political context is genuinely an obstacle to its power, as we see whenever some academic novelty escapes from the Ivy League onto the tabloid front pages and causes a scandal.

The final Left considered here, social-democratic parties, is the most significant one because it exercises actual political power in a number of major European countries, and in the European Union itself, and because it has traditionally been competent in delivering bread-and-butter policies to its urban voters. In recent years, however, social-democratic parties have fallen increasingly under the influence of middle-class public-sector radicals, adopted many of their cultural nostrums, and lost much of their traditional blue-collar electorate. They now find themselves falling into minor-party status. Nationalism and the nation-state are among the main reasons for their collapse. For these concepts directly clash with the Left's new preference for rational self-chosen identities over inherited "natural" ones, obstruct the achievement of its vision of human equality over national equality, and block the national and international redistribution of resources it now seeks.

National identity may be the most intractable of the Left's difficulties. Leftists of all kinds are extremely reluctant to accept that culture, language, and a shared history are vital supports for national community. They are viscerally unwilling to see open borders and the erosion of citizenship as threats to national cohesion. Indeed, they regard such fears as racist or xenophobic. To explain what holds the nation together, they offer two answers: liberal institutions and social-democratic transfer payments. Under liberal institutionalism, citizens are held together by a strong state which protects them and their rights. They therefore owe the state their loyalty. Yet, as Sir Noel Malcolm pointed out in his 1991 pamphlet on sovereignty, how strong is a state going to be if people are taught to think of it merely as a geographical area containing a certain number of human beings endowed with rights? Nations like the United States rooted in the principle of consent have traditionally taken great care to encourage the "Americanization" of newcomers, and for good reason.

According to the transfer payments theory, governments promote national solidarity by transferring resources from favored to disfavored groups and by encouraging all to participate in entitlement programs such as Social Security, which promote an ethic of equal citizenship. In sixties Britain, the London School of Economics' Professor Richard Titmuss delivered the pure socialist theory of national identity: the use of social services is a badge of citizenship. As long as the state has the fiscal ability to keep the checks coming, it can maintain solidarity even without the need for a shared identity rooted in culture and language.

It is not, however, as simple as that. We now know that taxpayers and voters are more willing to fund government transfers if they are linked to the recipients by the ties of sympathy and fellowship that exist in a shared national culture. The more diverse a society is, the less willing it is to spend money on welfare. That's the paradox of the welfare state, it needs national solidarity to finance national solidarity. And what if the treasury runs out? The costs of financial flows are rising because of aging populations and migrant services. Instead of sustaining national cohesion, transfer payments have already become a threat to it in countries such as Denmark, which has adopted a policy of "welfare chauvinism," i.e., generous safety-net programs available only to legal residents.

Social democrats respond to these pressures by such policies as closing tax havens, transforming trade agreements into vehicles for extending regulation, imposing taxes on international financial flows, "harmonizing" regulations in bodies such as the European Union, and so on. Eventually their governments form cartels—that is what the European Union is once its idealistic rhetoric is stripped away—to maintain monopoly prices for their services. But it is in vain: these new transnational bodies suffer from even worse defects than single welfare states: they are remote, undemocratic, and lacking even the semblance of a shared national culture. The overall result is the up-surge of populist nationalism across Europe, which is a protest against, among other things, the erosion of national sovereignty and demo-cratic accountability in the European Union.

Unfortunately for the Left, nationalism may be an insoluble prob-lem for them. Though some leftist intellectuals have argued for the adoption of a more patriotic stance (largely for electoral reasons) since Richard Rorty raised the issue twenty years ago, there is what William Voegeli in his recent *Law & Liberty* commentary on nationalism calls a "fundamental tension in the Left project between equality and community. Each is valued. In a perfect world, both would be fully realized. In the real world, however, there are no clear guidelines for synthesizing the two or for choosing between them when they clash." And clash they do. If your aim is to achieve global economic equality (over however long a time scale), then you will have to reduce the standard of living of Americans, including poorer Americans, below what it would otherwise have reached. If your priority is to raise the standard of living of the American poor, however, you will have fewer resources to devote to foreign aid to the world's poorest. And in either event you won't be able to tell the truth to your activists about the second course or to your voters about the first.

It's an agonizing dilemma, but perhaps a very academic one. For the experience of leftist regimes through history and around the world suggests that the likeliest result of an ideological socialist economic policy in the United States would be a reduction in American prosperity to the point where both foreign aid and domestic poverty programs would fall. And though unintended, that too would be an expression of the Left's idea of a decent patriotism: sacrificial utopianism.

The Enemy Is an Idea

MICHAEL ANTON

◆

T HE ENEMY is an idea—at least in part.

But who speaks of "enemies" anymore? Isn't the human race beyond such low, petty, potentially violent concerns?

No. It will never be. It cannot be. As long as there will be man, he will have friends and enemies—individual men no less than groups of men.

Lately a group of dishonest men have taking to dismissing this concern as "Schmittian," after the German political philosopher Carl Schmitt. But this is just their way of calling their own enemies "Nazis." These sophists forget—or deliberately obscure—that Schmitt's core insight follows Plato, who gives three definitions of justice in Book I of the *Republic*, the central being that justice is helping friends and harming enemies. Only this definition survives as Plato proceeds to elaborate his political philosophy.

Schmitt was a Nazi because he joined the Party, not because he understood that politics cannot be separated from—can never fully rise above—the friend–enemy distinction. Or, if believing in the friend–enemy distinction makes you a Nazi then Plato was a Nazi, too. As was virtually every thinker in the Western tradition. We expect this kind of malevolent lunacy from our leftist enemies but not from (former) ostensibly rightist friends. Therefore let this be understood: anyone who today dismisses the concept of "enemy" is himself an enemy, for he aims to deceive and, via that deception, to harm—either by design or out of delusion.

45

Our enemy—the idea of which I write—denies the existence of enemies. Like the devil, it is seductive and promises great goods. It preaches universal brotherhood, global unity, a "borderless world." Also like the devil, it has many names: liberal international order, rules-based international order, new world order, neoliberalism, among others. But its truest name is "universal and homogenous state" (UHS). To speak more precisely, the UHS is the underlying philosophic idea; the others are epiphenomena, attempts to make concrete in deed what the UHS prophesies in speech.

Under the rubric "liberal international order" (LIO), this idea has been much in the news lately. It is held to be an unalloyed good, the totemic structure of our time, the only thing standing between humanity and ruin. It is also said to be under constant attack from President Trump and his allies and friends. This latter claim is even true, depending on which understanding of "liberal international order" is meant, for there is more than one.

The concrete meaning of "liberal international order" is the collectivity of institutions created in the immediate post–World War II era. But what really matters are not just the institutions themselves but also—perhaps more so—the underlying philosophy or ideology that gave rise to them, plus their methods of operation.

The initial—and ostensible—purpose of the LIO in this understanding was to do for Europe (and Asia) what the Peace of Westphalia, the treaties that ended the War of the Spanish Succession, and the Congress of Vienna had done previously: end a conflict, reconcile enemies, and create decades of peace. In this respect, the LIO may be understood as one of many similar efforts in a long line: a temporary solution to a temporary problem, adapted to the particular circumstances of its particular time.

Occasionally statesmen are tempted to think more grandly of their present, and pressing, task and to dream of "making the world anew." And sometimes the settlement to a particular problem does, in fact, fundamentally change the world. The Treaty of Westphalia not only ended the Thirty Years War, it created an international system based on the principles of state sovereignty and foreign non-interference in domestic affairs that lasted centuries and that, in attenuated form, still stands.

The architects of the LIO held their own work in still higher regard. They, or many of them, thought they were building not merely for decades or even centuries but for all time. To this hubris was added another, and wholly new, element: ideology, the desiccated, doctrinaire codification of philosophy.

It's an unsettled—and perhaps unsettleable—question how many architects of the "liberal international order" thought of their project in these terms: permanent, unassailable, aligned with a new and superior understanding of nature. Did Jean Monnet intend his modest European Coal and Steel Community to become the European Union behemoth? Likely he did. But if so, it is a non-trivial detail that he declined to *say* so to the broader European public. Indeed, never having stood for elected office at all, he relieved himself of the bothersome necessity of having to explain his program to any but a handful of international elites, nearly all of whom supported it.

One architect of the LIO, however, never found circumspection either necessary or to his taste. Alexandre Kojève emigrated to France from Russia at an early age, a White fleeing the Reds. Which is ironic, given Kojève's later self-identification as a "Stalinist" and credible, if unproved, allegations that for thirty years he spied for the USSR.

Kojève is today known principally for three things. First is the influence of his famous lecture course on Hegel, taught in Paris in the 1930s and attended by a rogues' gallery of students who would go on to become some the most destructive intellectuals of the twentieth century, including Sartre, Lacan, Merleau-Ponty, Weil, and Beauvoir. Foucault and Derrida—too young to have attended the course in person—later claimed Kojève as a major influence. Though in fairness, it should be noted that Kojève's influence was not entirely malign. No less than Leo Strauss regarded Kojève as one of his few worthy philosophic opponents, and other attendees of those lectures included Queneau and the eminently sober Raymond Aron.

Second is the content of those lectures. In them, and in his subsequent writings, Kojève claims to have "fixed" Marx by bypassing him in favor of Hegel, whose own errors Kojève also claims to have fixed. Not a modest man, to be sure.

Third is Kojève's longtime work in the French bureaucracy, in a rather nondescript office under a vague title that belied his importance. One of Strauss's students, Stanley Rosen, described Kojève as "the Mycroft Holmes of France." That is, he was to the post-war French government what Sherlock's older, smarter brother was to the Victorian Whitehall: the decider. Except Kojève was real. Rosen quotes one of his favorite sayings: "De Gaulle decides on relations with Russia and the *force de frappe*; I, Kojève, decide everything else."

A central contradiction in Kojève's thought is his claim on the one hand to have "fixed" or moderated Marx, and his unapologetic Stalinism on the other. Certainly, Kojève tolerated and even excused Stalinist excesses in his own rhetoric. He seems to have taken Hobbes's dismissive comment that tyranny is merely monarchy disliked to mean that there is no fundamental distinction between just and unjust rule; there is only sovereign power or its lack.

And yet Kojève often seems to have gone out of his way to praise more "moderate" examples of his preferred polity in contrast to Stalin's USSR; for example, in his famous debate with Strauss, he held up Portugal's Salazar to show that Hegelian utopia need not rest on a foundation of (too much) terror. Something in him intuited that terror doesn't sell.

Many of us comfort ourselves with the thought that Marxism cannot be done "soft." If so, that would indicate that the means necessary to support it, because so brutal, will always be unpopular, making any Marxist regime unstable and short-lived. Tocqueville's famous warning about "soft despotism" seems not to apply, and not merely because it was penned decades before Marx wrote, but also because it describes a regime so much less harsh, less anti-natural than Marx's.

Yet Kojève's greatest "achievement" appears to have been to bridge the gap: to take what Tocqueville meant as a warning and to transform it into a recommendation. For the ancient philosophers, tyranny is a danger coeval with political life. Man can avoid it for a time—perhaps even for a long time—but we can never eliminate the possibility. When and where tyranny arises, the classics recommend mitigation, making the best of a bad situation. Essentially, they urge the tyrant—for his own good and for the good of the ruled—to govern like a legitimate king, to treat the polity as if it were his estate. At most they concede that some tyrannies are in a sense necessary in a "post-constitutional" situation after the breakdown of an established order, but are just only in the sense that deserved punishment is just.

Kojève turns all this—and more—on its head. Necessary mitigation becomes a positive good; deserved punishment is elevated into the "end of history"; and Marx's dystopia is reimagined as the "universal and homogenous state." Which is, in concept, exactly what it sounds like: universal (aspiring to cover the entire globe), homogenous (treating, and working to make, everyone the same), and a state (the world's sole wielder of sovereign power).

The philosophy underlying all this is deep and complex and—with one exception, explained below—needn't detain us here. It's the popularized version—the ideology—that matters, many of whose basic tenets will be instantly recognizable as the conventional wisdom of our globalist elites, the Davoisie:

Political and economic integration among states reduces causes of conflict.

Integration also reduces "friction" and therefore costs of doing business.

Integration leads to greater efficiencies in the allocation of monetary and human capital, and of other resources.

Integration is therefore always good, and the solution to almost any problem is more integration.

Diversity, inclusivity, and equity ("DIE") are necessary for integration to succeed and also are positive ends in themselves.

Only in an integrated environment—and therefore the more extensive the better—can these positive ends be achieved and maintained at their fullest.

These last assertions derive from Hegel's concept of "recognition," viz., that "history" is driven by the struggle of each and every person to achieve "recognition" of his/her/"their" (if ever there were a time to assault the English language with idiotic pronoun misuse, this would be it) personal claim to dignity by all other persons. In the ideologized version under which we currently live, that requires the mass redistribution of honors in the name of tolerance, fairness, and redress.

One can easily see the Marxist elements of this system: e.g., its universalism, insistence on leveling, the way it sees all history through the sole lens of past injustice or group struggle. Its most notable non-Marxist feature—its contempt of the proletariat and exaltation of an oligarchic ruling class—is explainable not merely by the desires of the ruling class (for every ruling class prefers to be rich rather than poor) but also by the clever way that neoliberalism has (mostly) substituted Marxism's redistribution of wealth with the redistribution of honors.

The qualifier is necessary, because some wealth redistribution still goes on—though not at the scale, or with the intent, anticipated by classical Marxism. Rather, the point under neoliberalism is to tie the "wealth" (however meager) of some to their allegedly retrograde refusal to grant "recognition" to others—specifically to the "diverse," the downtrodden, the "unincluded." This is why neoliberalism finds it permissible to celebrate the destruction of certain (let us call them Red State or "flyover" or "deplorable") communities. Like the peasant in Marxist theory, the modern "deplorable"—however penniless or powerless he may seem or believe himself to be—remains a stubbornly retrograde force who cannot be persuaded to abandon his "privilege" and so must be crushed.

We must not underestimate the appeal of this vision. It may sound dystopian and terrifying to us, but it is a source of inspiration and hope to millions. Some of those millions simply look past the necessary heavy-handed intrusiveness—the demonization, the propaganda, the censorship, the anarcho-tyranny, the double-standards, and various unfairnesses—on which the system must rely. Others relish these as features, not bugs.

But supporters of this new regime all agree that it offers at least one great good: the final, long-awaited, and much-longed-for coalescence of humanity (or at least the good parts) into one universal siblinghood. It's no accident that the official anthem of the European Union is Schiller's "Ode to Joy" as set to music by Beethoven (*alle Menschen werden Brüder*)—nor is it an accident that the European Union recently began an effort to criminalize the "denigration of the European Union and its symbols." Though one wonders how long the "gender-specific" language of Schiller's poem will be allowed to stand unexpurgated.

I wrote earlier of a contradiction in Kojève's thought. We find another nestled within the contours of neoliberalism. It is, as noted, universalist and seeks universal siblinghood for all humankind. It holds this to be the highest and most obvious good. It therefore does not know what to make of the hold-outs, those who like their particularity and don't want to give it up. Are such people simple flat-earthers?

In any case, how can one form a brotherhood with those who don't want to be brothers? But remaining with them or getting rid of them each poses a mortal threat to the project. Keep the deplorables around and they're likely to drag the polity in the "wrong" direction, toward nationalism and populism, away from neoliberalism. Kick them out, or separate from them, and you've admitted that your brotherhood has failed, its universalist pretentions are phony. The mere existence of hold-outs—whether inside your polity or outside in another one created for the purpose of holding out—is a standing rebuke that cannot be tolerated.

This (in part) explains the weeping over Brexit, Trump, the Yellow Vests, and the resurgence of nationalist politics throughout Europe. These acts of defiance are unwelcome signs that the vaunted "end of history" has not yet arrived, and worse, may *never* arrive. The only way to square the circle is to assume that they are manifestations of sabotage by "wreckers" who, once dispatched, will no longer stand athwart progress. Which is the operating assumption, for now.

Trump's signature sin is not merely to side with but to give voice to—to *lead*—the defiers. This is why his every word is condemned as a dangerous solvent on the supposedly unifying and stabilizing forces of globalization.

But if one begins from different premises—from a belief in eternal human nature—one understands the defiance differently, and is buoyed by it. Even on Hegelian terms, it's possible to understand the defiance precisely as arising from resentment of neoliberalism's refusal to "recognize" deplorables or their concerns. Yet a truer understanding would be that, while the deplorables do crave recognition, they do so not on Hegelian terms but on human terms. They wish to have their equal natural humanity recognized, of course, but also their status as husbands and wives, parents and children, brothers and sisters, co-workers and friends, and—last but not least—fellow citizens.

If we are to define a "deplorable" as a hold-out from neoliberalism, the LIO, and the UHS, then we may say that he holds out in part owing to his stubborn insistence on the ineradicability of the distinction between countryman and foreigner, citizen and alien, and—in the final analysis—between friend and enemy. There will always be nations, which means there will always be friends and enemies. Mankind is not, cannot be, and therefore will never be a universal brotherhood. To the neoliberal, this thought is retrograde. To the deplorable, it is not a thought; it is nature—no more to be despised or attacked than wished away.

This—I believe—inexpungible opinion among the larger portion of mankind is a great good, a reason for hope. It is a reason (one among many) why the project of universalist homogenization must fail—a failure to which anyone concerned with the fate of human freedom should look forward.

But this should not be taken as license for complacency. The fact of that failure's inevitability must not be allowed to obscure the vital point that *when* the failure occurs matters a great deal. The longer this goes on, the greater the toll it will take, and the harder our recovery will be.

This suggests the necessity of action, of resistance. That action can take many forms: spiritual, memetic, intellectual, organizational, political. But at the end of the day, to defeat an idea requires not just a better idea—which we have—but one marshaled in the service of a superior reality, a true and appealing vision of a real nation with real communities, real commonalties, real bonds of civic friendship, and a real sense of who we are, and who we are not.

We have that, too. Or, we used to. Our supreme and most pressing task is to remember it and get it back.

Liberty:
Collective & Individual

ANGELO M. CODEVILLA

◆

M Y PURPOSE here is to examine the philosophical and practical bases for the American people's rejection of the past century's peculiar "internationalism," and to suggest that the best way of transcending it, and hence to resume control of ourselves as well as of our relationship with other peoples, is to return to the principles set forth in the Declaration of Independence and practiced by presidents from George Washington to Theodore Roosevelt.

Our Declaration of Independence states as a self-evident truth that: "The laws of Nature and Nature's God" entitle "one people"—any and all peoples—to a "separate and equal station" "among the powers of the earth." Because all men are naturally free to distinguish themselves collectively among "the powers of the earth," therefore each people, being sovereign over itself, may exercise its natural liberty to rule itself, and only itself.

Biblical revelation of equal creation—"and God created man in His own image, male and female created He them"—is also the source the Declaration's other "self-evident truth": "all men are created equal . . . endowed by their Creator with certain unalienable Rights . . ." This truth is self-evident to those who believe that God creates all human beings, and that this Divine image is single, ineffable. Natural reason supports this truth. Consequent to it, because each and every human being is naturally sovereign over his own "life, liberty, and the pursuit of happiness," no one may rightly rule another without his consent.

The *collective* right of peoples to have lives of their own and to pursue happiness as they see fit, is simply the writ-large version the equal rights of *individuals* that proceeds from their equal creation. Though individual liberty implies collective liberty, the exercise of collective liberty does not necessarily imply the enjoyment of natural human rights, never mind the exercise of civil liberties. These liberties happened to coincide in America, albeit imperfectly, because of a heretofore happy coincidence of a certain sense of nationhood with a certain understanding and dedication to righteous living.

As far as America's Founders were concerned, the whole point of government is to preserve the happy coincidence that made America unique. John Quincy Adams explained the Founders' America:

> the people . . . were associated bodies of civilized men and christians, in a state of nature, but not of anarchy. They were bound by the laws of God, which they all, and by the laws of the gospel, which they nearly all, acknowledged as the rules of their conduct. They were bound by the principles which they themselves had proclaimed in the declaration . . . by all the beneficent laws and institutions, which their forefathers had brought with them from their mother country, by habits of hardy industry, by frugal and hospitable manners, by the general sentiments of social equality, by pure and virtuous morals.

The people, he said, were to cultivate and show forth a character, commitment, and cohesion peculiar and separate from that of other nations:

> It is a common government that constitutes our country. But in THAT association, all the sympathies of domestic life and kindred blood, all the moral ligatures of friendship and of neighborhood,

are combined with that instinctive and mysterious connection between man and physical nature, which binds the first perceptions
of childhood in a chain of sympathy with the last gasp of expiring
age, to the spot of our nativity, and the natural objects by which
it is surrounded. These sympathies belong and are indispensable
to the relations ordained by nature between the individual and
his country. . . . These are the feelings under which the children
of Israel "sat down by the rivers of Babylon, and wept when they
remembered Zion."

The precondition for preserving the American people's unique
character was and would remain preserving its independence—
its collective liberty to govern itself. Because the habits that come
from exercising responsibility, collective as well as individual, are
key to that character, making that exercise the foremost priority
for all policy is essential. America-centeredness does not mean na-
vel-gazing. It does mean looking at everything through the prism
of what serves America.

Classic American foreign policy

"America First" may be the most succinct description of George
Washington's statecraft. By telling his fellow citizens "the name of
AMERICAN, which belongs to you, in your national capacity, must
always exalt the just pride of Patriotism, more than any appellation,"
he was adjuring Americans to look at the rest of the world through
America's prism. Washington had no doubt that his country would
soon be powerful. But maintaining its peace and independence would
depend less on power than on regarding everything from an American
perspective. From that perspective, all nations are equal, in that their
interests and quarrels are their own, not ours. Our interest is to have
"Harmony and liberal intercourse" with all those who would have it
with us. To do that, we should "observe good faith and justice towards
all Nations." That, in turn, requires avoiding political connections that

would drag us into their quarrels. Taking sides in others' divisions naturally tends to divide Americans against one another. Said Washington: "Why forego the advantages of so peculiar a situation? Why quit our own to stand upon foreign ground?"

The 1790s had taught Washington that commitments to foreign nations embitter existing domestic partisan divisions. Because each side in our domestic quarrels may cite foreign concerns to strengthen its case against other Americans, alliances tend to be sources of weakness, not strength.

When Washington wrote to the nation's governors that it was now up to the American people to "establish or ruin their national Character forever," he was urging Americans above all to guard their identity as a virtuous people. In the tradition that Montesquieu and Gibbon had transmitted from Livy, Washington repeatedly reminded Americans that, to remain free, they must take care to be virtuous. Never in history had that been easy. Nor would it be now. America would become powerful. But no power would make up for lack of virtue. Maintaining the integrity of America's soul was also the reason why John Quincy Adams emphasized abstinence from others' quarrels, from the temptation to make America "the dictatress of the world."

Adams was intimately acquainted with Washington's teachings, with Hamilton's, Madison's, and Jay's reasoning on what it takes to maintain peace, as well as with his father's application of naval power to carry this out. This, in addition to his having watched as Presidents Jefferson's and Madison's neglect of military power forced America into the War of 1812, led him to devote his diplomatic career to defining and establishing the Founders' foreign policy as a paradigm for future generations.

Expansion of U.S. territory in North America, mutual non-interference and reciprocity, and deadly force against pirates and importers of slaves were among his policy's pillars. Adams regarded the 1819 Transcontinental Treaty that secured an internationally recognized U.S. border on the Pacific Ocean, in addition to the accession of Spanish Florida, as his proudest achievement. Earlier, he had successfully argued for military action to destroy bands of British-led terrorists operating out of there. John Quincy Adams's formulation of the Monroe Doctrine is a perpetual reminder of America's geopolitical priorities. Since the peoples on our borders and the nearby islands are the agents by which both good and ill may come to us, U.S foreign policy must begin with a defensive focus on them. What is nearest is of dearest concern.

Adams's central concern, however, was securing the American people's exercise of their collective liberty among nations—in short, ensuring self-government. Taking unilateral responsibility for actions vis-à-vis the rest of the world was a necessary but not sufficient condition for that. Since any and all commitments to foreign powers comport restrictions on one's collective liberty, concern for that liberty requires minimizing commitments.

He also advised minimizing formal commitments; diplomatic experience had taught him that governments do what they believe to be in their interest, regardless of the existence of agreements that command or forbid. Understanding that diplomacy is the verbal expression of realities, he relied on making sure all sides understand how each other's interests interact. He explained Washington's insistence on reserving alliances for specific circumstances by pointing out that although sovereign nations' interests may coincide from time to time, they are never identical. America's own interest, overriding geopolitics and commerce, is to strengthen its own very peculiar, fragile, republican character. Adams hoped that acting honorably and respectfully among nations would also help foster honor and integrity—republicanism's bases—among Americans.

Safeguarding self-government and promoting responsible behavior was also Abraham Lincoln's theme in the 1838 Young Men's Lyceum address. He too did not fear foreign aggression. Irresponsibility, however, would open the way for men of "the family of the lion, the tribe of the eagle"—men like Napoleon, who would impose the order that Americans could not or would not exercise on themselves.

Progressivism negates collective liberty

By contrast, our progressive ruling class believes that concerns with matters purely American are obstacles to mankind's peaceful progress. Doing well by America, they believe, is a function of doing our primary duty to the international community. Hence our ruling class has focused foreign policy on matters beyond ordinary people's ken and expressed it in jargon, in no small part to remove what they do from ordinary people's hands. They believe that Americans' instincts mix isolationism and militant nationalism and lead to war.

Contemporary internationalism, however, is less about policies than it is part of a larger progressive effort to substitute government by officials, supposed to be intellectually and morally superior, for representative government by of and for the people. Depriving the American people of collective liberty—with regard to matters foreign as well as domestic—is Progressivism's overriding proximate objective.

From society's commanding heights, a ruling class of intellectuals, churchmen, politicians, publicists, industrialists, and bureaucrats has devalued the attachments to God, family, locality, and nation by which Westerners, and especially Americans, have lived, and it has purveyed in their place the sense that we are parts of a world political economy run by experts. Attempting to delegitimize popular dissent, this class labels "populism" ordinary people's efforts to interfere with their sovereign judgment, to assert who they are, collectively and individually. The suffix "ism" occludes the dictionary meaning of the word "people" with a sinister implication. By identifying democracy with the "institutions of democracy" that they control and by pinning an invidious label on the people, who they do not control, the ruling class claims that the people's rejection of their rule, the assertion of rule by the *demos*, is "undemocratic."

Nevertheless, this ruling class touts its own commitment to "democracy"—which is nothing if not rule by the people.

The assumption that human beings are rightly governed only by their betters entered the progressive tradition as an inheritance from France's *Ancien Regime*, which Napoleon had institutionalized throughout Western Europe under the banner of the French Revolution. Hegel celebrated state-engineered progress as the march of the human spirit. Only in the 1880s, in the writings of Josiah Strong, Woodrow Wilson, and Herbert Croly, did this assumption come to America. The domestic objectives at which Progressivism aims are such that ordinary people can hardly imagine them. Progressivism's international objectives—perpetual world-wide peace and the equality of peoples—are even farther from ordinary people's grasp or cares. The Administrative State internally, and "globalism" internationally, are two sides of the same progressive coin.

Sorcerers' apprentices, and us

Popular rejection of the persons and ideas that have ruled the Western world for much of the past hundred years reopens fundamental questions about how we should live our lives, collectively as well as individually. What should this rejection mean for Americans? The following contrasts the priorities of today's ruling class and those of the people whom it purports to represent, with a focus on international affairs.

Woodrow Wilson took America to war in 1917 to try to improve the world. The American people never signed up for that. In 1919 and since, they bitterly rejected that notion. But neither then nor since have the American people's preferences outweighed our bipartisan elites' desire to wield America's enormous power on the international stage. As these elites minimized the people's collective liberty regarding international affairs, they made a mess of things.

Theodore Roosevelt had synthesized the previous century's foreign policy in the formula "speak softly and carry a big stick." His emphasis on balancing ends and means matched the American people's appreciation for solvency in personal and business affairs. For him, the most dangerous of habits was to "combine the unbridled tongue with the unready hand." Progressive policy, however, has been insolvent—bankrupt—because its words have been such that no amount of earthly power could match them. Foreigners' belief in American power far in excess of its application has given progressive policy such efficacy as it has had. But endless discrepancies between words and deeds have made American power increasingly incredible and contemptible.

Since words can neither change reality nor cause foreigners, whose interests differ from America's, to share in our officials' departure from it, we should keep in mind that the American people are the only ones whom our officials' unbridled tongues can deceive.

Even though the description of progressive U.S. foreign policy as "liberal hegemony" dates only to the 1990s, the sense that American power and wisdom entitles—nay, obliges—U.S officials to lead, order, and sheriff the globe has been their lodestar for a hundred years, regardless of the public's very different concerns.

Because progressives' transnational or multi-lateral objectives are foreign to the American people, they have largely removed power over foreign policy decisions from the people by making commitments through executive agreements or by acting informally. Following Woodrow Wilson, they have pressed their priorities on the American people by pretending that these reflect our allies' demands. Prioritizing alliances over objectives, they have made it difficult to evaluate those objectives.

Progressives have treated international "institutional norms" as if they were international law binding on Americans. Those institutions—notably, the United Nations, the European Union, NATO, and the complex of committees thereof—have become our foreign policy establishment's ends in themselves. "Internationalism," too, has become something of an end in itself, as may be seen in a proposal by

Germany and France to establish an "Alliance for Multilateralism," ostensibly directed at no one but aiming to foster what it calls a "rules-based order." The proposal's language hints not at curbing anything that China, Russia, or Iran might be doing, but rather at curbing an American desire to protect America's own interests and identity. Thus do latter-day "multilateralists" around the world ally with progressive Americans against the American people.

By the same token, members of America's progressive establishment have lived profitable careers by advising and helping likeminded foreigners in their public and private affairs, and by enjoying foreigners' assistance in their own private and public affairs in America. The latter includes all manners of help or hindrance in business and political campaigns. This confusion of foreign and domestic affairs, as well as of the public and the personal, has corrupted its practitioners in every imaginable sense of the word.

While abjuring war as a tool for securing national interests, progressives have used the tools of war in the name of ideals. Dealing with matters of the utmost seriousness, they have acted unseriously.

The U.S armed forces are the world's largest and, by many measures, the world's best. And yet the U.S has lost its wars since 1945. The "war on terror," having cost some eight thousand of our military dead and five times that number crippled, plus perhaps six trillion dollars, leaves us with multiples of the number of terrorists arrayed against us than when it started. Were our armed forces to be engaged against Russia or China on the Niemen River and in the Western Pacific, respectively as current plans call for, they would be defeated. That is because our progressive establishment is mismatching forces and objectives, means and ends, as it has done in the War On Terror, in Vietnam, and in every military confrontation since 1950. Its refusal to defend U.S. territory against missiles, especially from Russia and China, leaves no doubt that U.S nuclear policy is bluff advertised as bluff, and that our nuclear forces deter only ourselves. The American people have paid—are paying, will pay—the bloody price.

Most important, the U.S. government squandered the American people's trust. America is left over-armed and insecure, over-allied and increasingly opposed. This is what happens to a country when the civil and military officials, academics, and publicists responsible for leading the nation take leave of ordinary people's concrete concerns to focus on their fancies as well as on their personal and corporate interests. Americans now are subject not to men of "the family of the lion and the tribe of the eagle," but to self-indulgent bureaucrats, as presumptuous as they are incompetent.

Who wants what?

Today's progressive establishment, having pursued its dreams with plenary power, yet seeing those dreams turn into troubles they had not imagined, now focuses its energies on maintaining its prerogatives against an increasingly assertive public. Specific issues of policy having become of secondary importance, power itself—who rules—is the issue. The public's interest in regaining self-governance and in preserving what is left of its identity is the reverse of that same reality.

In our time, the progressive establishment's substantive causes are a pale reflection of themselves in their heyday. Nobody today refers to the UN as "the last, best hope of mankind." Not in a half century has anyone in authority suggested that it might be possible to eliminate war. Yet these were the tropes of the mid-twentieth century. Bureaucratic inertia sustains feeble attempts at "arms control," as well as occasional references to "nuclear non-proliferation." Today, nobody would bet his money that any nuclear power might be persuaded to "de-nuclearize." And yet, the idea that nuclear weapons were in the process of being dis-invented animated the Clinton, Obama, and both Bush administrations. Who, today, would recite George W. Bush's 2005 inaugural with a straight face? Who would argue that alliances must determine missions rather than the other way around? The "Arab Spring" was all the rage in Washington in

2011. And then it raged. The European Union is a done deal—that is in the process of undoing itself. Not so long ago, the notion that this progressive project would be the other end of a "dumbbell" of transatlantic power was catnip among the great and the wise. Now it just looks dumb.

The establishment merely repeats mantras. "We are the hub of alliances unrivaled in the history of nations," said Barack Obama. "Our strength as a nation is inextricably linked to the strength of our unique and comprehensive system of alliances and partnerships," echoed General James Mattis, Trump's Secretary of Defense. They confess them catechetically because they sense they are hollow.

Policy is not what absorbs the establishment's energies. Their concern is social and personal. It is holding on to their places of profit and prestige against the American people's rejection of themselves and their whole caboodle, foreign and domestic. They act to weaken whoever disrespects progressives. The Washington Post's Jennifer Rubin spoke the mind of many establishmentarians: "these people are not fit for polite society. I think it's absolutely abhorrent that any institution of higher learning, any news organization, or any entertainment organization that has a news outlet would hire these people."

Hence, establishment media, in unison, have been publishing and airing, not descriptions of policies, but attempts to associate those who disagree with them with repulsive things. On behalf of The Washington Post's Jeff Bezos, Robert Kagan published a ten-thousand-word article that previewed his book The Jungle Grows Back, in which he deemed "populism" synonymous with "isolationism," "protectionism," and "resistance to immigration." He had already written of Trump's election with the leading question: "is this how fascism comes to America?" Stanford's Larry Diamond wrote in The Wall Street Journal: "in one country after another, elected leaders have gradually attacked the deep tissues of democracy—the independence [from the voters] of the courts, the business community, the media, civil society, universities, and sensitive state institutions like the civil service, the intelligence agencies and the police." Voting against the establishment, you see, is undemocratic!

Fascism, stupidity, racism, sexism, and every phobia imaginable are now the establishment's standard explanation for ordinary Americans' refusal to pay them what they consider due deference.

What do "populists" want? No more or less than what the Declaration of Independence proclaimed: the exercise of our collective liberty. That is populism's defining demand. Who rules? "We the people" get to rule ourselves. "Institutions" have no right to rule. Neither does social position or group identity confer any such right. If there is such a thing as a crime against popular government, government by the people, it is the presumption that some are more equal than others.

If there had been doubts that, at least in America, the exercise of collective liberty is the precondition for exercising individual liberty, our progressive establishment's vindictive presumptions to the contrary should settle those doubts.

Imagine All the People of Color

Social justice & identity politics

DAVID AZERRAD

◆

To the casual observer, the professed goals of contemporary identity politics appear unassailable. Who, after all, wouldn't want to build a more inclusive democracy? How could anyone oppose granting rights to the oppressed, the marginalized, and the stigmatized? As a student once asked me, incredulously, "Isn't it better to love than to hate?"

The appeal of identity politics is further reinforced by its powerful morality tale. After confronting us with the injustices visited upon women, black people, homosexuals, and any other number of victimized identity groups, social justice arbiters then claim for themselves the exclusive mantle of justice. On the one side are the baddies who are at best unaware of America's structural inequities and their own unearned privilege, or at worst just plain bigoted. On the other side are the good guys, the identitarian coalition of the "woke" and the "oppressed" fighting for social justice. You're either a racist or an anti-racist. *Tertium non datur.*

Cracks, however, soon begin to appear in the colorful mural of identity politics. The progress of social justice, it turns out, always comes at the expense of certain core natural and civil rights. Freedom of association had to be sacrificed to end discrimination. Free speech will suffer the same fate if hate speech is to be eradicated. As will due process rights for men accused of rape if #MeToo has its way. More "rights" for more people, it turns out, also means fewer rights for some people. The language of love and inclusion is particularly deceptive in that

67

it gives cover to a deeply intolerant mindset. Like all ideologues, identitarians brook no dissent. They are quick to silence and impugn the motives of those who disagree with them. They periodically indulge in Two Minutes Hate against any number of Emmanuel Goldsteins who deviate from the accepted script when speaking of aggrieved identity groups. They reserve particular fury for women and minorities who eschew the victim mentality and dare to think for themselves. Tolerance, in truth, is extended only to those who already subscribe to the tenets of identity politics. And so the demand for diversity produces mind-numbing conformity—as is readily apparent in our identitarian institutions of higher indoctrination.

The manifold contradictions of identity politics invite us to look beyond the misleading kumbaya rhetoric and examine its actual end goals. There is one question in particular the identitarians are careful to avoid as it goes to the heart of their project. Identity politics has clearly identified the most privileged, bigoted, and therefore problematic identity groups that together prop up the oppressive American regime: primarily whites, but also men, and the non–LGBTQ, i.e. straights and so-called "cisgenders." These oppressor groups intersect to produce the straight white cis-male who is blamed for almost all of the world's ills. Identitarian social justice, like all forms of justice, demands that the guilty be punished. What then is to be done with this Great Straight White Cis Male Satan and the defining elements of his identity?

Statistical parity

Many reasonable people will surely immediately object to such an incendiary way of framing the issue. There is no movement calling for the elimination of straight white cis-men—much less of straights, whites, men, or cisgendered individuals. The *New York Times* writer Sarah Jeong's old tweets—#cancelwhitepeople—have thankfully not yet caught one.

Indeed, in their public presentation, the identitarians join most progressives in simply calling for the various groups that comprise our diverse nation to be represented in all realms of life in proportion to their percentage of the total population. Social justice would culminate not in the elimination of any one group, but in a world where roughly 96 percent of the desirable positions in American life are held by cis-gendered heterosexuals, 60 percent by non-Hispanic whites, and 49 percent by men (or whatever the percentages may be in the future, given changing demographics).

"A truly equal world," the billionaire Facebook executive Sheryl Sandberg explained to us in *Lean In*, "would be one where women ran half of our countries and companies and men ran half of our homes." Long before her, Martin Luther King, Jr., had already posited that "if a city has a 30 percent Negro population, then it is logical to assume that Negroes should have at least 30 percent of the jobs in any particular company, and jobs in all categories rather than only in menial areas."

Widespread tacit acceptance of this principle of statistical parity fuels our national obsession with leveling disparities and closing gaps of all kinds. "Only 35 percent of African American lesbian and bisexual women have had a mammogram in the past two years, compared to 60 percent of white lesbian and bisexual women," the Center for American Progress has noted with alarm.

In studying these different group outcomes, identitarians increasingly permit us only one explanation: bigotry. Any other explanation—whether it be biological, cultural, volitional, or stochastic—is *prima facie* ruled out and denounced as racist, sexist, homophobic, or any of the other terms used to stymie inquiry and silence dissent.

Ibram X. Kendi's reductive treatment of the subject in his best-selling *Stamped from the Beginning: The Definitive History of Racist Ideas in America* is revealing of the broader identitarian mindset. Kendi, a historian at American University and the youngest person ever to win the National Book Award for nonfiction, opens his massive tome by defining as racist "any concept that regards one racial group as inferior or superior to another racial group *in any way*." Readers are therefore forbidden from the outset from making any comparative generalizations, and Kendi encourages us to apply his dogmatic pronouncements on race to other protected classes

Kendi is, in effect, demanding that we silence our rational faculties. He wants to confine the mind to a chaotic world of particulars, never allowing it to ascend to the general, where it might recognize patterns and aggregate differences. Not just reason, but humor too must be sacrificed at the altar of Kendian anti-racism. No Frenchman, Jamaican, and Chinaman—which is not the preferred nomenclature—may ever walk into a bar again.

Kendi's argument rests on two dogmatic assertions. The first is that race is in its entirety a social construct. There cannot be any genetic component to explaining racial disparities. Kendi's refusal to entertain such arguments is understandable. Discredited racial science has in the past been used to defend a hierarchy of races and, in the extreme, to justify slavery and genocide. But to acknowledge the biological dimension of race need not have this sinister character. Natural human equality is not based on natural human homogeneity. Natural rights are no more predicated on genes than they are on I.Q., height, birth order, or income. One can permit science to acknowledge the biological dimension of race while upholding the dignity of man and the civic equality of all Americans.

Most Americans, myself included, would prefer not to talk about such matters. The findings of science are liable to misinterpretation. They are bound to offend some and stoke the pride of others. But the ever-ubiquitous principle of statistical parity, along with the ever-more draconian measures taken to enshrine it, leave us no choice. Science must be called in to defend the republican principle of equal rights under equal laws for all citizens, regardless of life outcomes. This can be done in a responsible way, making an allowance for nature, while eschewing biological determinism.

Kendi's second unexamined and unproved assumption is that "All cultures, in all their behavioral differences, are on the same level." They are all "equal in all their divergences," in his Orwellian turn of phrase. Why, then, do they differ so markedly in life outcomes for their members? For Kendi, there can only be one explanation: racial discrimination. It "is the *sole* cause of racial disparities in this country and in the world at large." Or, as he explained to *The New York Times*, "when I see racial disparities, I see racism."

Oddly, nowhere in his five-hundred-page tome does Kendi ever see racial disparities between Asians and whites. If he did, he would have to conclude that based on income and educational attainment, America is in fact an Asian supremacist nation which discriminates against whites—unless they are Ashkenazi Jews—and blacks—unless they are Nigerians.

Ultimately, Kendi's expectation of statistical parity is groundless. The default setting in a liberal, pluralist, and free society that spans a continent is diversity—not in the superficial sense that has currency today, but in the deeper sense of diverse preferences, abilities and subcultural norms that necessarily yield a great diversity of outcomes, both *within* groups and *across* groups. The Madisonian extended republic, let us remember, was *designed* to promote a "great variety of interests, parties, and sects."

Genuine diversity will be even more pronounced in a multicultural society such as ours, which encourages cultural separatism at the expense of assimilation into a mainstream. Here, for example, is Kendi's vision of what a "truly multicultural nation ruled by multiculturalists" would look like:

[It] would not have Christianity as its unofficial standard religion. It would not have suits as its standard professional attire. English would not be its standard language or be assessed by standardized tests. Ethnic Studies would not be looked upon as superfluous to educational curricula. Afrocentric scholars and other multicultural theorists, lecturing on multiple cultural perspectives, would not be looked upon as controversial. No cultural group would be directly and indirectly asked to learn and conform to any other group's cultural norms in public in order to get ahead.

How this heterogeneous whole is supposed to produce uniform outcomes across all its constitutive components Kendi never bothers to explain. In fact, he seems completely unaware that his celebration of authentic multiculturalism contradicts his demands for statistical parity. The more different we're all encouraged to be, the more we'll all be the same. Or so his logic goes.

But why would we expect the many "communities" that make up our multicultural republic to succeed and fail at the same rates in the same realms if they value different things, cultivate different virtues and have different visions of the good life? As Thomas Sowell never tires of pointing out, even identical twins raised in the same family don't turn out the same. If the most conformist monocultural society imaginable will not produce equal outcomes, then neither will a multicultural one.

That is why enforcing the principle of statistical parity requires levels of social engineering, thought control, and expropriation that would make Big Brother blush. In the most horrifying passage in *Stamped from the Beginning*, Kendi calls for "creating an agency that *aggressively* investigates the disparities and punishes conscious and *unconscious* discriminators. This agency would also work toward equalizing the wealth and power of Black and White neighborhoods and their institutions." Lest we worry about the totalitarian implications of granting the state complete jurisdiction over our minds and our property, Kendi reassures us that his Department of Anti-racism would only be staffed with "formally trained experts on racism" (such as himself, presumably) and "no political appointees."

It is a testimony to the power of identity politics in America that Kendi can make such totalitarian demands without bothering to argue on their behalf and that almost no one has called him out for it. Imagine by contrast what would happen to someone who had the temerity to suggest that irreducible biological differences place limits on what men and women can do.

There is no basis in reality for asserting that discrimination is the only reason, or even the primary reason, why statistical parity is not a reality—especially in 2020. Human nature being what it is, discrimination will never be fully rooted out from the heart. It has, however, been considerably attenuated in the past two generations. In many areas, it has been completely eradicated—at least in its traditional form (the *bien pensants* and the courts do permit discrimination, but only against men, whites, and Asians). Corporate America, universities, and all levels of government have increasingly made it their mission to achieve diversity—often at the expense of maximizing profits, imparting knowledge, and serving the public.

Beyond parity to diversity

Even if, for the sake of the argument, we were to concede that statistical parity is both just and achievable, we still could not help but notice that no one in America—especially not the identitarians who claim to be most committed to eliminating disparities—seems to care about disparities that cut against whites, men, or heterosexuals.

The "gender pay gap" has received more attention than the Kennedy assassination, but how many moral crusades have been launched to eradicate the violent death gap, the life expectancy gap, the sentencing length gap, the workplace accident gap, or any other of the many other gaps in which men fare much worse than women? Aside from Christopher Caldwell, has anyone else noticed that non-whites gained 10 million jobs, while whites lost 700,000 during a nine year-period that roughly spanned the Obama administration? And who among us has heard of the gay and lesbian premium (on average, homosexuals earn significantly more than their heterosexual counterparts)?

We all know that, for all the talk of parity, there can be never be too many women, people of color, and LGBTQ people in the desirable realms of life. Nor can there ever be too many men, whites, or heterosexuals in the non-desirable realms of life. The principle of statistical parity is, in reality, applied selectively as a cudgel against oppressor groups. The real goal of identity politics thus proves to be not proportional representation, but greater diversity, i.e. fewer whites, fewer men, and fewer heterosexuals. For that is all that "diversity" means: fewer members of the bad groups. How few we are never told, but fewer than we currently have is always an imperative. Beyond that, the term "diversity" is essentially meaningless. It tells us nothing about the actual composition of a group.

Each year, for instance, the Institute for Diversity and Ethics in Sport releases a racial report card for professional sports leagues. The more people of color—whatever their color may be, so long as it's not white—the higher the grade. So the NBA gets an A+, even though its roster is less than 20 percent white in a country that is 60 percent white.

Although it is almost never explicitly said, everyone knows that straight white men contribute nothing to diversity. In fact, they undermine it, thus leading to the paradox that an office with no straight white men would be considered more diverse than an office with some straight white men (the only exceptions to this rule are all-black neighborhoods or schools—because of the suspicion of racism—unless the school in question is an HBCU).

. . .

The primacy of diversity over parity is further confirmed by the barely restrained jubilation with which the media and the Left greet news of America's impending demographic transformation into a so-called "majority-minority" country.

In 2015, for example, Vice President Joe Biden celebrated America's "unrelenting stream of immigration"—specifically Muslims, Africans, Asians, and Hispanics: "It's not gonna stop, nor should we want it to stop," Biden enthused. "As a matter of fact, it's one of the things, I think, we can be most proud of." In his excitement, Biden moved up the date of the demographic tipping point by almost three decades:

> Folks like me, who are Caucasian of European descent, for the first time, in 2017, will be an absolute minority in the United States of America. Absolute minority. Fewer than 50 percent of the people

in America from then and on will be white, European stock. That's not a bad thing. That's a source of our strength.

This demographic trend line—what has been called "the browning of America"—is presented to America's white majority as a just dispensation from above to which all must submit. America will be made less white. There is nothing you can do about it. Nor should you want to do anything about it, since a less white America will be a better America—whites being responsible for slavery, Jim Crow, the Trail of Tears, the Chinese Exclusion Act, Japanese internment camps, and the systemic racism that defines the country to this day. The fewer whites, the more diversity, the better the country, the world, and the planet.

Any attempt to slow, halt, or—heaven forbid—reverse this demographic trend line is, of course, denounced as racist. Only a racist would oppose the rapid demographic transformation of his country—unless that country is non-white, in which case it should be opposed lest it overwhelm the native people and their traditional culture. Western nations, being mostly white, are not afforded this right.

Any policies that delay—even by a few years—America's demographic tipping point are also fiercely opposed, regardless of whether they were intended to do so. In early 2018, for example, the Trump administration proposed to reform the country's immigration laws and to secure the southern border. No mention of demographics or race or ethnicity was made in the plan itself or in its public presentation.

Then–House Minority Leader Nancy Pelosi immediately denounced the whole effort as part of "an unmistakable campaign to make America white again." *The Washington Post*, after conducting its own analysis of the plan, concluded it would delay the tipping point by up to five more years. "By greatly slashing the number of Hispanic and black African immigrants entering America, this proposal would reshape the future United States," Michael Clemens of the Center for Global Development told the *Post*. "Decades ahead, many fewer of us would be nonwhite or have nonwhite people in our families. Selectively blocking immigrant groups changes who America is." America, in other words, is defined teleologically by its *future* demographic composition—not its past or its current population (or its founding principles). It belongs not to all its citizens, but to the future progeny of its nonwhite population. They are who we are.

The national push for greater diversity in matters of race will not of course come to a stop once non-Hispanic whites are reduced to a minority. If diversity has a limiting principle, it has yet to be stated. That is not to say that diversity does not have a limit. It does. For all their denunciations of whites, the identitarians remain strangely drawn to them. Louis Farrakhan hates white people and wants nothing to do with them. Our identitarians hate white people but want to be around them.

Many are themselves white and generally preach diversity more than they practice it, especially regarding the neighborhoods in which they live and the schools to which they send their children. Wokeness for them is more performed than lived. This is most readily apparent in the academy, where no single tenured white professor has yet to resign his position to make way for a professor of color.

As for the non-white identitarians, in particular the black ones, many embrace a strange form of neo-segregationism. They want to live, study and work among whites—but to do so with the possibility of escaping their company when they choose. They want segregated integration. As Georgetown University professor Michael Eric Dyson has observed:

Those of us who are integrationists want our cake of mainstream values. But many of us want to buy it from a black baker and eat it in a black restaurant in the black section of town. Others of us want our racial separatism. But we often want it in mixed company: a black dorm at a white university, a black history month in a predominantly white country, and a black house in a white suburb.

In order to appease its people of color, America must therefore maintain a sufficient number of whites to sprinkle around their schools and neighborhoods. Identity politics does not, in the end, promise a future without whites, although it does not censor eliminationist rhetoric either. The white race may well be "the cancer of human history," in Susan Sontag's memorable formulation, but this is one cancer we do not want to cure. We just want to reduce the size of the tumors and distribute them more evenly across the body.

. . .

Identitarian social justice demands America become not only less white, but also less straight. This will not be done through immigration (although the Obama administration's repeal of the HIV travel and immigration ban was hailed as victory for diversity), but by creating an ever more accepting climate that allows people to express their hitherto stifled sexual identities.

That is why news of the rising number of Zoomers and Millennials who do not identify as straight is always greeted as sign of progress. "It is heartening to see the future of this country loosen the shackles of traditional identities and unapologetically embrace who they are," GLAAD President Sarah Kate Ellis explained after her organization published a survey claiming that 20 percent of Millennials identify as LGTBQ.

For the time being, most identitarians still adamantly maintain that sexual identities are natural and not chosen (for those keeping track, science must deny that races exist, but affirm that the elusive gay gene does). This presumably sets an upper limit on how gay America can become. But cutting-edge academic queer theory rejects all "essentialist" accounts of sexuality: it argues that homosexuality is as socially constructed as heterosexuality.

On questions of sex, identity politics ultimately converges with the sexual revolution, whose ultimate promise is polymorphous perversity—the celebration of unbridled sexuality. The full emancipation of sexuality would seem to require us to abandon all constrictive identities—from gay to straight, including bi—and follow our urges wherever they may take us. Liberation, in the fullest sense of the word, points to a world in which all have become omnisexual.

. . .

The invocation of diversity to reduce the percentage of whites and straights in the American population obviously cannot be applied to men. Nature has remained deaf to the cries of radical feminism and continues to produce slightly more than one male baby for every female baby. The problem, according to modern feminism, however, lies not with the natural existence of the Y chromosome, but with the socially constructed masculine gender. As Simone de Beauvoir might have said, one is not born a man, one becomes a man. Sex may be a given, but masculinity can be—and must be—deconstructed and ultimately abolished. As must femininity. Justice demands that we transcend gender altogether.

In a post-gender world, neither men nor women would be nudged, pressured, or forced to follow scripted gender roles. All would be radically free to choose. But rest assured, they would all freely choose the same! These genderless but sexually differentiated humans, would still end up being proportionally represented in all realms of life. How this will happen without coercion in spite of vast differences in body size, brain chemistry and hormonal makeup has yet to be explained. Perhaps a "fourth wave" of feminism can study the question.

In the meantime, preferential measures and re-education into androgyny are necessary to ensure statistical parity between men and women. A relentless stream of propaganda must encourage women to silence their feminine longings and set their sights on competing with men for money and honor. The boys, meanwhile, must be stuffed with Ritalin and have their spiritedness extinguished. Those who submit to the gynococracy will be rewarded in the wokeplace. *Whoever thinks otherwise goes voluntarily into the madhouse.*

Deconstructing whiteness

The emasculation of men, the promotion of sexual perversion and the flooding of America with Third World immigrants are necessary but not sufficient to achieve identitarian social justice. Even then, a rump of whites will still remain. And though they will have been reduced to a minority who are no longer overrepresented in all realms of accomplishment, they will still be white, with all the psychological and historical baggage this entails.

Whiteness itself will therefore have to be deconstructed. Whites will have to understand that race is a historical and social construct with no basis in nature. They will have to learn, as the clerics of wokeness are fond of saying, that race itself is racism. Or, as Rachel Dolezal, cursed be her name, has explained: "racism creates race."

America, the identitarians explain, has constructed arbitrary racial categories to justify its oppressive rule over others. Whiteness may not be real by nature, but it has been made real. There is no biological white race, but there is a social white race. And it "consists of those who partake of the privileges of white skin in this society," as John Garvey and Noel Ignatiev explained when launching their journal *Race Traitor* whose motto was "Treason to whiteness is loyalty to humanity."

Whites must therefore be taught to acknowledge their privilege, repent for the sins of their race, adopt a deferential pose vis-à-vis the people of color who continue to be oppressed by the pervasive whiteness of America and actively oppose racism. In his *Sermon to White America*, Dyson intones: "The most radical action a white person can take is to acknowledge this denied privilege, to say, 'Yes, you're right. In our institutional structures, and in deep psychological structures, our underlying assumption is that our lives are worth more than yours.'" Whites, in short, must learn their place.

By contrast, so-called "people of color"—as the term itself implies—are never asked to deconstruct their blackness, redness, yellowness, or brownness. Their races are no more real than the white race, but they are encouraged to take pride in and celebrate the achievements, real or fake, of their colored brethren across history. Racial solidarity is encouraged as a means to bring down the structures of white oppression.

Identity politics thus both denies and celebrates race at the same time. It cultivates guilt, repentance, and self-flagellation in whites, while promoting pride, aggrievement, and vindictiveness in non-whites. It teaches race for me, but not for thee. And it encourages all to hate the accursed white race. As the father of Black Power, Stokely Carmichael, long ago urged, we must "fill ourselves with hate for all white things."

And if we do this long enough, then one day we may perhaps reach the promised land of racial reconciliation. Kendi ends his interminable history of racism by reassuring us that there "will come a time when we will love humanity, when we will gain the courage to fight for an equitable society for our beloved humanity." Michelle Alexander concludes *The New Jim Crow* with an impassioned plea "to cultivate an ethic of genuine care, compassion, and concern for every human being" and to build "a thriving, multiracial, multiethnic democracy free from racial hierarchy."

Paradoxically, the way to do this is not by transcending race, but by paying even more attention to it. Racial harmony will come not through colorblindness but through "a *permanent* commitment to color consciousness," according to Alexander. In other words, the more we focus on race, the more we entrench into our laws a racial caste system, the more we see racism everywhere, the more we relentlessly attack whites for their privilege and in so doing, unwittingly develop their racial consciousness, the more we allocate desirable positions on the basis of race rather than merit, then the more likely we are to all get along one day.

Identity Politics in effect invites us to embrace racism, but to do so in the name of anti-racism. And it asks us to believe that this anti-racist racism, because it is in the service of a good cause, will not lead to a race war, but instead will heal our divisions and bring us closer together. Herein lies the fundamental contradiction of identity politics. It speaks of love, but fans the flames of hatred.

There is no reason to believe that whites as a group will suddenly be viewed positively or forgiven for the sins of their father if their numbers decline to some arbitrary level or if they learn to hate themselves enough. Hatred, once its take hold of the soul, does not readily give way to forgiveness and reconciliation—especially not outside of a Christian theological context. The Reverend Martin Luther King could forgive. Ibram Kendi cannot—nor does he want to.

America & the International Order

CHRISTOPHER BUSKIRK

◆

L AST YEAR, the French sociologist Emmanuel Todd wrote that "the opposition between what are called populist movements and movements of so-called elites has long been complicated by a major paradox: the elites express, in elegant and apparently moderate terms, absurd ideas that are characterized, in reality, by extreme violence. The discourse of globalization is nothing but…shit in a silk stocking." Forgive the expression. It is how Napoleon referred to his foreign minister, the Duke of Talleyrand, and is thus a useful allusion in this context. Todd continues: "Among its propagandists, we find well-bred persons who boast of every imaginable university credential, but who say awful things and condemn a significant part of the population to social exclusion. In the opposing camp, we find improbable personalities, such as Trump, who certainly utter obscenities, but obscenities that are in fact much more reasonable and moderate in their economic, social, and demographic implications."

Talleyrand was the richest man in France and her chief diplomat. Today he would be a "Davos man"—a member of the global elite that gathers every year in Davos, Switzerland, for the World Economic Forum. He took bribes from France's enemies even as he was negotiating treaties on behalf of Bonaparte. Such betrayals are not just the stuff of history—they still happen. Samir Jain was the U.S. National Security Council senior director for cybersecurity policy during the Obama Administration. He worked in the West Wing of the White House for the president, making him one of the top— perhaps *the* top—American official in charge of cybersecurity. This man now works for the Chinese, having taken a position advising the mobile communications giant Huawei on how to "deal with" (or, more likely, evade) the security standards he helped develop. This is wrong. But it is typical of the global elite that sees itself not as American or French or Brazilian but as rather as a class of free-agents, seeking their own narrow, parochial interests concerned with what lines their pockets regardless of what it does to their countries. The spirit of Talleyrand is alive and well in America.

Perhaps we should not be surprised. The bipartisan neoliberal ideology that is the basis of the post-end-of-history bipartisan consensus permeated all of human life with market ideology, places where it was never supposed to go, and in the process denying essential aspects of human life and human nature: family, religion, order, belonging. All of these things, which conservatives have historically viewed as fundamental to human life, were subordinated to theories of competition. And through the implementation of this ideology—one that I argue is inhumane—we transformed America from a nation of citizens to an empire of laborers and consumers.

Still, despite the sense that something isn't right, most people— especially the sort of upper-middle-class professionals who think about these things—assume that life has been getting consistently better. But what if that were just a conceit that we tell ourselves to avoid facing hard truths? Then what? What are the social and political implications of failing to meet our Embedded Growth Obligations? And how does that affect America's place in the world and the peace and prosperity of the nation?

American foreign policy, including trade policy, since World War II has been guided by the principles of the Atlantic Charter, which was issued jointly by the United States and Great Britain on August 14, 1941, and was signed by Franklin Delano Roosevelt and Winston

Churchill. Some have argued that Churchill agreed to the Charter, which mandated the rapid deconstruction of the British Empire after the war, under duress as a precondition for American assistance without which Britain might have succumbed to Germany. The essence is undoubtedly true. And it's a fitting start to the postwar order, in which the victor nations used hegemonic power to impose a new world order motivated by utopian liberal internationalist ideology.

The Atlantic Charter, for example, was the precursor of the United Nations, and of the General Agreement on Tariffs and Trade (which evolved into the World Trade Organization that has been the prime vector of deindustrializing the United States and the exportation of American middle-class jobs to Asia). The Atlantic Charter also led to the formation of NATO, which, while useful when facing the threat posed by the Soviet Union's multi-decade efforts to facilitate Communist-government takeovers all around the world, has since become a United States–subsidized welfare program for European governments that decided to let Americans fight optional wars on their behalf while their citizens get ten weeks vacation during the summer. To be sure, I don't oppose lengthy French vacations—that's one of the beautiful things about France. I'd rather the American middle class were doing that than spending another summer in Iraq or Afghanistan.

The first thing for Americans to recognize is that the liberal impulse and the globalist impulse—they are closely related—strongly diverge from America's historic self-conception, from historic American foreign policy, and from our posture towards the rest of the world. These impulses are wildly ideological, presumptuous, naïve, idealistic, and mostly wrong. And they have wrought our current world. Is there any important measure on which the trajectory of American or Western civilization can be said to be improving? Let's look at some concrete examples.

Religiosity is declining. The churches of Western Europe are empty. Even America is not immune. We may just be lagging behind the European experience. The much-discussed rise of the "nones" (that is, Americans who answer "none" on surveys of religious belief) in the United States is real. According to a study by the Pew Forum, nones now account for 26 percent of the population. They are a larger group than Roman Catholics (20 percent) and are closing in on Protestants at 43 percent. Church attendance has been steadily declining since the Great Depression, but as recently as the late 1950s nearly half the country attended church services every week or nearly every week. Today it's between 38 and 40 percent, and that number is buoyed by the higher percentage of older Americans who regularly attend church. Only 28 percent of millennials are regular church attenders.

Birth rates are low and mostly declining. The replacement fertility rate is 2.1 children born to every woman in her lifetime. Throughout Europe the total fertility rate ("TFR") has collapsed and every country has a TFR well below the replacement rate. For example, in Germany it is 1.60, in Norway 1.68, in Sweden and France it is 1.85. Americans thought until recently that we might escape the baby bust, but the U.S. fertility rate fell to 1.77 in 2019. In 2010, with the economy still in the doldrums and millions of home foreclosures still putting Americans under significant economic pressure, the TFR was 1.97 but even with the economy now growing, fertility has continued its decline. What can one say about a nation that does not want to, or cannot afford to, even replace its own people with the next generation?

Let me be blunt: we live in a largely materialist, self-centered, pornified culture. Social media itself bears many of the features of pornography. Women have been told that work out of the home is liberation and fulfillment itself, while having children and raising a family in the home are slavery or, at best, demeaning, unpaid drudgery. As though the majority of women would leave the home for careers, would "Lean In," and suddenly become Sheryl Sandberg, the billionaire CEO of Facebook. Go ahead, wait until you're in your thirties to start a family and have children. You can have it all! The reality is that most women aren't Sheryl Sandberg—and few want to be.

Many have great jobs that they enjoy. But plenty work at Walmart or in a cubicle in an office and are just trying to make ends meet. And of course, biology doesn't care about ideology. Female fertility begins to decrease dramatically at the age of twenty-eight. Think you can freeze your eggs? Not so fast. The results aren't great and women don't find this out until years later.

Of course, men aren't any better off. Men are the butt of the joke in the current year. Masculinity is "toxic." Fatherhood is the fountainhead of the much maligned patriarchy. And what passes for masculinity in popular culture is a degraded and profoundly immature caricature: fat guys spending their weekends watching other men play sports on TV while guzzling junk carbohydrates processed in toxic vegetable oils that promote the very inflammatory diseases that shorten lives and tax our healthcare system. And their cultural intake is comic book movies. The only acceptable expressions of masculinity are immature, deracinated replays of early adolescence.

Add to this the toxic combination of the hookup and #MeToo cultures and you have a society in which men and women are alienated from one another and, in the worst cases, are openly hostile.

But there's also an economic aspect that is at least as troubling. Household formation is much more expensive today than it was fifty years ago relative to income levels. Real wages (seasonally adjusted) have remained essentially flat over the past fifty years. There has been some much-needed improvement over the past few years, but there is much, much more needed. How have families made ends meet? By adding an additional income. In 1970, roughly 30 percent of families were two-income households, but by 2018, it was over 63 percent. The key point here is that today it takes two incomes to support the needs of a middle-class family, whereas fifty years ago it took one. In strictly economic terms, that means it takes twice as much labor outside of the home to support the same family of four. And that means that the raising of children—when children are present at all—is increasingly outsourced. That's not improvement.

Americans' paychecks are bigger than 40 years ago, but their purchasing power has hardly budged

Average hourly wages in the United States, seasonally adjusted

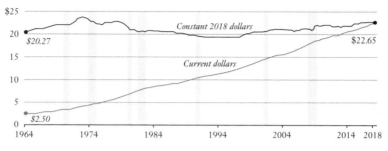

Note: Data for wages of production and non-supervisory employees on private non-farm payrolls. "Constant 2018 dollars" describes wages adjusted for inflation. "Current dollars" describes wages reported in the value of the currency when received. "Purchasing power" refers to the amount of goods or services that can be bought per unit of currency.

Source: U.S. Bureau of Labor Statistics.

Pew Research Center

One of the driving factors has been housing prices. Housing has become much more expensive relative to wages and consumes a larger share of income. This is especially true in the top twenty largest cities where most young people have clustered for work. Millennials have a very difficult time buying a home, which for young people is a key part of starting a family. You're not going to get married and have kids if you're sharing an apartment with three friends. It doesn't work. This has led to less household formation and fewer children. But it also contributes to atomization, loneliness, materialism, decreased social trust, and increased reliance upon government. If you're not thinking about the next generation, you're really just thinking about how to amuse yourself until you shake off this mortal coil—it's essentially suicidal.

In light of growth in GDP since the end of the Great Recession and the decade-long stock market boom one might reasonably argue that we are living in uniquely prosperous times. And in a real sense that's true. But it also tells us less than we think because the rise in asset prices has disproportionately benefited the baby boomer generation. At the same time, data show that every generation after the baby boomers is much less wealthy than the Boomers were at their age. In other words, Gen Xers own a much smaller share of national wealth per capita at age fifty than boomers did at age fifty, just as they did at age thirty-five. Meanwhile, millennials own a smaller share of national wealth than the Gen Xers did at age thirty-five, meaning that they are way behind the boomers.

Looking at American prosperity from another angle, it's indicative of the nation's substantial wealth that we have an epidemic of obesity, not hunger. However, it's harder to buy a home, which is a vital indicator of people's prosperity. Food is cheap and plentiful, but housing is expensive and in large cities it is increasingly scarce. Overall, our material conditions have been flatlining for a long time and the dissatisfaction and social unrest has been in part papered over with amusements, including on-demand streaming media, social media, legal marijuana and opiates, and internet pornography, which accounts as much as 30 percent of all internet traffic.

What's worse is that our GDP growth is misleading. It measures consumption, which is a single measure of "economic activity." But the public in general and policymakers in particular routinely conflate GDP with wealth. In a society that was not as deeply dependent on debt that would be more accurate, but it's not now. As a result, much—maybe all—of GDP growth is the result of massive increases in debt and the concomitant debt-fueled spending of the federal government. Some economists are realizing that GDP measures—and thus incentivizes—the wrong things.

For instance, a parent who takes a job outside the home and installs the children in a nursery or with a paid nanny has a double-impact: the increased economic activity resulting from the parent's and the caregiver's jobs. When this occurs en masse, as it has over the past fifty years with a much higher percentage of women entering the workforce, there is a necessarily corresponding increase in GDP. "Hurrah!" the financial press will say when the data come out, and politicians will clamor to claim credit for it. But is that sort of economic growth really producing more prosperity and better lives? Isn't that what economic growth is supposed to be for? Is society better off with fewer children and with more of them being raised by hired help rather than their mothers? How much that is crucial to society is lost by removing parents from the home?

And at the same time that the government has been on a debt-fueled spending binge, consumers have done the same thing, piling on auto, home, credit card, and student loan debt with uniquely American alacrity. Since the 1980s, the time when the federal debt began to blossom, consumer debt has also ballooned. Why? There is no point in getting into a discussion of character, the decline of traditional Protestant notions of thrift, or dewy-eyed nostalgia. They are important but too imprecise and they are unnecessary when concrete, well-defined economic realities will suffice. In short, people have had two reasons for weighing themselves down with previously unimaginable levels of debt: because they can and because they must. That is to say, that the economy is currently structured so that most wage-earners make barely enough to get by and they fill in the gaps with abundantly available consumer debt which, owing to lenders mostly correct assessment of default risk, charge them high interest rates which in turn creates a debt trap. This is not unlike the situation in which the federal government has placed itself, the signal difference being that consumers cannot create fiat money to pay their debts. According to a survey by Chase Bank, 40 percent of Americans would have serious difficulty covering $400 in emergency expenses. It's impossible for a society that wants to maintain self-government to sustain such a situation for long. The political incentives and necessities simply won't allow it.

Changing the economy so that the broad middle class can afford to remain solidly middle class on a single income must be a national priority. It will require a different kind of economic growth than we have had. There are two basic ways to get GDP growth without relying upon debt-fueled spending: population increases and productivity growth. Productivity is essentially a measure of technological advancement: we switch from horses to cars, from typewriters to desktop publishing, from analog to digital. But productivity growth has been anemic because we are in the midst of a massive stagnation in technology that has lasted for half a century or more. Yes, everyone has a smartphone that is connected to the internet. Those both represent great advances. But they are not enough and that's why we don't see the growth in productivity numbers. What's more, there are good arguments to be made that many of the apps that have fueled the sense of technological advance, such as Twitter, Instagram, Snapchat, and the Chinese-government-owned TikTok, are actually destructive. And this leaves aside the massive increase in serious addiction to pornography.

Here are just two examples of the great stagnation in technology.

The average speed of a commercial passenger jet in 2019 is actually *slower* than it was in 1965. Most jets today cruise at a speed of around 480 to 500 knots. The Boeing 707, which was a standard passenger airliner in the 1960s, cruised at 525 knots. The major advance has been a marginal improvement in fuel efficiency. We don't even have the Concorde anymore. If you had asked someone in 1965 what jet travel would have looked like in 2019, they would surely have predicted that, at a minimum, supersonic air travel would be the standard and that there was probably some form of hypersonic air travel. In reality, it takes us roughly the same amount of time to get from Los Angeles to New York, but we do it in dramatically less comfort. And if you're flying from LAX to JFK you are flying between two run down, dilapidated airports that were models of the then-nascent jet age, but are today national embarrassments that demonstrate all too clearly the unfulfilled promises and unmet embedded growth obligations that underlie American expectations.

Worse than the fact that jet air travel failed to progress the way its early innovators expected, life expectancy hasn't improved much since the early twentieth century. For all of the money we spend on science and healthcare, when you factor out improvements in infant and early childhood mortality, life expectancy has not improved all that much in the past century. A study in the Journal of the Royal Society of Medicine says that in mid-Victorian England, life expectancy at age 5 was 75 for men and 73 for women. For comparison, the Social Security Administration said in 2016 that American life expectancy at age 5 is 71.

The improvement in infant mortality is real and important. And it is something for which we should be profoundly grateful. But it's also the result of breakthroughs like vaccines and antibiotics that happened a very long time ago. So today, if you make it to five years old, your life expectancy is not that much different than your great-grandfather's. This is one of the embedded growth obligations that isn't working out. Science, especially in healthcare, was supposed to be making people live longer and healthier lives. And what's really crucial is that while life expectancy— a statistical average—has generally improved, lifespan—a measure of how long humans can generally be expected to live—hasn't. According to popular perception, the ancients all died very young. But that's ahistorical. Pliny tells us that Cicero's wife Terentia lived to 103. A 1994 study of looks at 298 famous men born before 100 BC who were not murdered, killed in battle, or by suicide, and finds that their average age at death was 71.

What's more, recent research shows that not only are we not living longer, we are less healthy and less mobile during the last decades of our lives than our great-grandfathers. This points to a decline in overall health. So for example, we have drugs to treat Type I diabetes, but why do we have so much more Type I diabetes than we did? We have drugs and procedures to treat cancer, but we also have more cancer. Something has gone very wrong.

The same rot can be seen in a number of other metrics:

• *Personal Income.* Many people have commented on the stagnation in median real wages that started in the early 1970s, but this statistic understates the problem. "In 1985," writes Oren Cass, "the typical male worker could cover a family of four's major expenditures (housing, healthcare, transportation, education) on 30 weeks of salary. By 2018 it took 53 weeks. Which is a problem, there being 52 weeks in a year." That's a huge decline in income. How have families made ends meet? Most families have found that they need two incomes to get by and they supplement with consumer debt.

• *Personal Safety:* Violent crime has nearly doubled over the past fifty-five years. In 1965, there were 1.99 violent crimes per 100,000 Americans, versus 3.81 in 2018. And it's worse when you look at some of the most horrible crimes. Reported cases of forcible rape, for example, rose roughly 350 percent from 23,410, a rate of .12 per 100,000 to 139,380, a rate of .426.

• *Family:* Virtually everything that measures the health of the most fundamental building block of society—the family—evidences serious corrosion. Out-of-wedlock births were 8 percent of the total in 1964 compared to 40 percent in 2014. This is not a peculiarly American problem; the United States is at about the middle of the pack internationally. In Chile, the out-of-wedlock birthrate is 70 percent. The number of children raised with no parent in the home after school—who are thus largely on their own for much of their childhood—has skyrocketed.

• *Deaths of Despair:* There has been a particularly disturbing spike in suicides. Suicide rates for people between the ages of fifteen and sixty-four rose 33 percent between 1999 and 2017, from 10.5 per 100,000 to 14 per 100,000. Why? The story of the modern world is one where history has ended, where we have entered into an era of universal peace, and where technological wizardry provides an endless array of amusements and diversions. Just look at everyone on Instagram: they're all good looking, smiling, happy. Social media is our Lake Wobegon, where all of the children are above average. And it's just as real.

• *Education:* More Americans complete high school and go on to college than ever before. But are they better off? Is American primary, secondary, or university education better than it was fifty years ago? Better how? I would suggest the following metrics: Are students learning what they need to learn to be good citizens? Are students learning the skills necessary to support themselves and a family on a single income? Is our education system good at selecting elite students—that is to say the best and the brightest—and cultivating them for leadership in science, art, and politics? In other words, do we have a strong, dependable system for creating and perpetuating national elites that can be trusted to protect and promote the interests of the entire nation rather than just their own? Even a cursory look at elite failure from Enron to Boeing to the loss of trust in media and government tell that tale. Is a college degree a better or worse deal financially than it was fifty years ago? To ask these questions is to answer them.

Wendy Brown describes the post–World War II neoliberal project as "the economization of all features of life." Professor Brown critiques neoliberalism and its discontents from the Left, but she brings to her analysis some sound observations. In too many ways the "conservatism" of the neoliberal post-War era allowed itself to be defined primarily by its anti-Communism. That was the glue that held the political coalition together. However, libertarianism smuggled Marx's economic view of life into American "conservatism" and thereby undermined its essential vitality and link to both religious and natural law traditions that were its historic basis. It made some important counter-arguments, but it fought the battle on the enemy's terms. For example, George Stigler, the Nobel Prize–winning Chicago economist who helped found the Mont Pelerin Society, wrote extensively about inserting the price system into politics. But reducing politics to markets is an essentially Marxist, inhumane, false view that degrades both life and politics. It takes a useful theory of markets—of the truly economic aspects of life—and tries to over-realize its implications as a Grand Unifying Theory that is in fact is cramped and dehumanizing. It reduces human society to nothing more than a series of utility-maximizing trades.

By accepting this view, political conservatism lost its essentially national character and identity until very recently. In response to the Marxist challenges America faced from communist imperialism, conservatives became over-dependent on ideology. But true conservatism is essentially much more practical. Its vitality comes from a view of life that recognizes the primacy of the family, the uniting power of religion, and the risks to both of expecting too much from politics. Protecting those two basic human institutions so that they are free to thrive and to act in their roles is the primary role of good government. There are, of course, other important functions of government, and whatever government does must be done well and with integrity, but that means eschewing utopian projects, focusing on what can be done well, and restoring a sense of obligation that places the wellbeing of American citizens above every other interest. But that's only possible by restoring a more sensible and realistic approach to politics.

Conservatives came to view the world too much in terms of theory; as a result they left reality—and the needs of actual Americans—behind. Political theory became a blinder and an impediment in far too many cases. They stopped asking the simple questions—"what's good for our people?," "is this working?"—and asked instead how well a given policy conformed to a theory of government. Questions like "does this promote free markets?" and "does this promote democracy abroad?" are abstractions. Free markets and democracy in other countries should be directly instrumental in expanding and sustaining the wellbeing of the average American, not religious totems pursued as though their promotion bought eternal salvation. That must stop. Politics is the practical art of getting and using power wisely. America acquired great power in the world, but like trust-fund kids unsure where they came from or what it took to get where they are, our politicians have not used our political power wisely. Competing ideologies of utopia have instead caused them to misspend America's fantastic wealth.

Utopia, we should recall, means, roughly, "nowhere." It doesn't exist. Politics on the other hand, is—or at least should be—relentlessly practical. Are my nation and my people better off or worse? Are we safe and secure? Does this or that action lead to peace and prosperity or conflict and poverty?

Asking those simple questions regularly would ground elites in the real world and provide a check on the human impulse to control. The sin of Eden, the desire described in Genesis 3:5 to be like God, is the first and most consistent sin. What was Babel but a shot at an impossible man-made utopia?

America is at its best when it eschews the politics of abstraction that inevitably promote sterility, corruption, and self-harm, and instead focuses on enhancing the real-life interests of her citizens. Is the middle class large, secure, and self-sustaining? Can average people afford to buy a home and have children?

American vitality and American national restoration go hand in hand. That means a connection to other Americans that is based on a shared history, common bonds, and a shared future. Citizenship itself is based on common ties of religion, of family, and of friendship. As George Washington said in his "Farewell Address," "the name of American, which belongs to you in your national capacity, must always exalt the just pride of patriotism more than any appellation derived from local discriminations. With slight shades of difference, you have the same religion, manners, habits, and political principles." It's easy to think that Washington's observation is less true than ever, but it's a guide for the way forward.

So if America is going to continue to play a large and beneficial role in the world, we must first restore and reinvigorate our own national identity. Washington himself is an example, but we could also look at Achilles and Patroclus. They present an ideal of friendship and trust and what friends can achieve. America can achieve much, too if we reorient away from short-term materialism towards a restoration high-culture based upon mutual responsibility and strong social ties that rely upon the family as both the model for society and its basic building block.

Suicide by Ideology

DANIEL McCARTHY

◆

JAMES BURNHAM begins his 1964 book *The Suicide of the West* with an arresting image. He tells of one day opening an old historical atlas and browsing through its maps that showed the expansion and contraction of one civilization after another: Assyria, Persia, the Greeks under the Macedonian leadership of Alexander the Great and his successors, Rome. Arabs forged into an empire by Islam, Mongols, and Turks had their turns, as did the various Germanic barbarians who overthrew the Western Roman Empire. Slowly the shapes of a post-Roman Western civilization began to emerge and grow—and continued to grow through to the end of the book. "The last map in my atlas' Western series—a double-size inserted page is needed for it," Burnham wrote, "is entitled, 'Colonies, Dependencies and Trade Routes, 1914'; and there before your eyes you can see at once that in A.D. 1914 the domain of Western civilization was, or very nearly was, the world."

Then Burnham closed the atlas and tried to imagine the maps showing the next fifty years, a half-century marked by the conquests of Communism in Russia, Central Europe, and East Asia and by the liquidation of Western Europe's colonial possessions around the world. "The trend, the curve, is unmistakable," he concluded. "Over the past two generations Western civilization has been in a period of very rapid decline, recession, or ebb within the world power structure" as judged purely by geography. By that simple and easily visualized criterion, Western civilization was undergoing contraction. Whether one characterized this contraction as "decline" or "decay" or employed any other value-laden term was less important than recognizing the underlying phenomenon itself, which was indisputable.

What was also indisputable was that no outside force had militarily defeated the West or overawed it with greater wealth or technological prowess. The contraction was of the West's own choosing. Arnold Toynbee had argued in *A Study of History* that most civilizations come to an end not by murder—being destroyed from without—but through suicide, which can be said to start when expansion stops. So Burnham argued that the West was suicidal, and the ideology of liberalism, thoroughly triumphant in the United States and Western Europe of the mid-1960s, was a rationalization of this self-murderous impulse: the ideology of Western suicide.

But Burnham, who died in 1987, did not live to see the end of the Cold War, the extinction of Soviet Communism (if not the East Asian varieties), and the unprecedented global prosperity brought about under Western and particularly American leadership over the last three decades. Was this "suicide"? Was it "contraction"?

In point of fact, yes it was: for even in the midst of these favorable strategic and material conditions, the West has not meaningfully expanded and has only lost ground culturally and demographically in its own homelands. Western military excursions into Afghanistan and Iraq have not succeeded in "Westernizing" those countries in any but the most superficial ways, while immigrants from non-Western cultures are today largely responsible for propping up population figures in the West itself.

If anything, "the suicide of the West" has taken on a more literal meaning in the fifty-six years since Burnham published his book. All Western nations—including the United States, the United Kingdom, and every member state of the European Union—have fertility rates that are below replacement levels. This by itself is not a problem unique to the West. What is unusual is the West's reliance on immigration as a substitute for its citizens' fecundity. Japan's population is shrinking, yet the Japanese prefer to turn to mechanization rather than immigration to mitigate the inconveniences. China has dwindling fertility levels, yet rather than accept demographic and cultural change through immigration, Beijing has embarked on renewed efforts to subjugate and either assimilate or extirpate the Uighurs, Tibetans, the people of Hong Kong, Christians, and many other ethnic, cultural, and religious minorities. China's ruling class is evil, but it is murderous, not suicidal.

Liberalism, as the rationalization of Western suicide, is today as strongly aligned with mass immigration, multiculturalism, and a deliberately alienating criticism of the West's own national and religious history as it once was (and still is) aligned with decolonization. The moral relativism employed by liberals of Burnham's time and earlier in support of removing Western influence (as well as Western control) from non-Western cultures is now giving way to a morally absolute condemnation of the West's heritage, which is increasingly labeled by liberals as "white supremacy" pure and simple, as well as Christian bigotry, Islamophobia, transphobia, sexism, and an endless count of other -isms and -phobias.

For Europe, the danger of combining an anti-Western liberal ideology with low domestic fertility rates and generous policies toward immigration and refugees is that more population will be drawn to the states of the European Union from the Middle East, North Africa, and Sub-Saharan Africa (where fertility levels are still high) than those states can tolerate while maintaining their historical religion, culture, and political character. What liberals may intend as a merely humanitarian policy and a post-Christian form of the confession of one's sins has the potential to lead to regime transformation. Far from pointing the way to "the end of history" in the form of a universalized and homogenized bureaucratic state, the European Union may be ushering in the end of Europe and the return of traditional religious and tribal divisions—only not the religious and tribal divisions of the West, but rather those that are traditional in the global

South and Near East. Those few European politicians who show an awareness of the hazard and urge measures to address it are, significantly, identified as "illiberal."

The United States does not confront the same geographic demographic predicament. Yet here too the suicide of the West has taken on acute new meanings. Life expectancy for Americans fell every year between 2015 and 2017, before recovering slightly in 2018, the most recent year for which figures are available. The recovery has been attributed to some success in confronting the opioid crisis. Other measures, however, indicate that "deaths from despair" are continuing to increase, with suicide rates, which have been growing relentlessly for twenty years, reaching record new levels in 2019. Americans have lately found the pain of living so great as to be worth risking their lives to end, or even worth ending their lives to escape.

While the United States enjoyed prolonged economic growth after the Great Recession, cultural and political indicators have shown a loss of confidence in God and country. Fewer Americans are identifying with any religion, and fewer of those who do identify with a religion are identifying with Christianity. In taxpayer-supported research universities, professors and administrators have recently come under federal investigation for accepting undisclosed funds from foreign sources, including for trading American technology to China. Google canceled an artificial intelligence project for the Pentagon in 2018 over employees' ethical concerns about working with the U.S. military, but the company and its personnel happily cooperate with Beijing.

Even the most basic manifestations of loyalty to one's own country cannot be taken for granted in the academy or corporate America. But a commitment to liberalism, in either its free-market form or its culturally leftist one, or both, may safely be assumed when dealing with America's moneyed and credentialed elites. Michael Bloomberg's 2020 presidential aspirations suffered irreparable damage from allegations of harassment and sexism. They were not

scuttled from the outset by his declaration in September 2019—
two months before he entered the presidential race—that "Xi Jin-
ping is not a dictator. He has to satisfy his constituents or he is not
going to survive."

Western geographic expansion had come to an end a half-century
before James Burnham wrote *The Suicide of the West*. In the half-
century and more since the book's publication, the West has experienced a reproductive arrest within its own borders combined with a
cultural tendency toward intense self-criticism and a greater open-
ness to influence from rival nations and civilizations. Although Western, specifically American, military power has undergirded what has
lately been called the "liberal international order," and though the
West has materially prospered under that order, liberalism remains,
as it was in Burnham's day, an ideology of national, religious, and
civilizational suicide. The question, now as earlier, is why the West
has chosen to contract, and what, if anything, can be done to give
Western nations once more a reason to live.

In Arnold Toynbee's telling, the suicide of a civilization often
begins with a war. In the case of classical Hellenic civilization, the
war was the Peloponnesian War, which not only pitted city against
city within the Greek world but class against class within the cities.
Although Hellenic culture would spread more widely in the years
and decades after the conflict, thanks to the conquests of Alexander
the Great, the kingly empires Alexander's successors would thereaf-
ter rule lacked the artistic and political spirit of the old city-states;
they were large but decadent. Rome did not subsequently overtake a
Greek civilization at its apex but one that had already lost its cultural and, ultimately, its martial vitality.

Toynbee similarly attributes the fall of the Orthodox Christian civilization of the Eastern Roman Empire to a war that long preceded the
military disasters that are usually cited as the cause of its ruin: in his
account, not the sack of Constantinople during the Fourth Crusade
in 1204 nor the capture of the city by the Ottoman Turks in 1453 but

rather "the great Romano-Bulgarian war of A.D. 977-1019" was the fatal occasion: "This fratricidal conflict between the two Great Powers of the Orthodox Christian World at this time did not come to an end until one of them had been deprived of its political existence and the other had suffered wounds from which there is good reason for saying that it never recovered."

A civilization entering its decadent phase may also give rise to a universal state and a universal religion, the one produced by the dominant minority or ruling class, as it seeks to make its power permanent at the cost of political calcification, the other produced by the empire's proletariat as they retreat from worldly commitments—hopeless political ones in particular—and seek transcendence instead. The transformation of the Roman Republic into the Roman Empire and the empire's subsequent Christianization stood as the paradigm of this case for Toynbee.

These are artful interpretations of history, and one might be tempted to see parallels to them in the development, or degeneration, of the West. The two World Wars of the early twentieth century are plausible candidates for the conflagration that signals the end of the Western genius and the onset of disillusionment. The European Union and the United States, as twin pillars of the vaunted "liberal international order," might together appear to constitute a universal state, though no universal religion has arisen among the masses. The pattern loosely fits, if only because it is so subjective. But why did the horror of the two World Wars have to lead to suicidal self-doubt, when the triumph of the victorious nations of the West might have led more self-confidence rather than less?

In *The Suicide of the West* Burnham refrains from giving a fully developed explanation of his own for the civilization's turn toward self-annihilation. He suggests that a loss of religious faith may be partly responsible. His earlier book *The Machiavellians* (1943) holds further clues. There Burnham considers the political consequences of conflict between two tendencies in the human psyche. Following Vilfredo

Pareto, he refers to these psychological complexes the "residues" that remain when rationalizations and other analytical distractions are removed. "Class I" residues involve "the instinct for combinations" and stand in contrast to "Class II" residues, which are characterized by "the persistence of aggregates." Persons in whom Class I residues are predominant have a love of novelty and may be deficient in loyalty; many of them are intellectuals. Those in whom Class II residues are most pronounced have a strong adhesion to existing groups and traditions, or as liberals today like to say, they exhibit "tribalism."

Burnham applies a metaphor from Machiavelli (who in turn reappropriated it from Cicero) to label these typical personalities as "foxes" and "lions." The foxes are characteristically more comfortable resorting to fraud, the lions with employing force. Both an individual and a state need a mix of each tendency, a balance between them.

Conditions of peace and prosperity allow foxes to thrive, at least at first. The traits of the lions become less valuable when there is little need for fighting, and indeed the spiritedness that distinguishes their type of personality may be disruptive within a peaceful yet dynamic society. Foxes are natural entrepreneurs; lions are pained and distressed by the transformation or outright destruction of the old "combinations" of human beings—social groups—or ideas. In a culture of experimentation and innovation, lion-like people are not only apt to underperform, they might be seen as obstacles to progress.

Before it became the ideology of Western suicide, liberalism was the ideology of foxes like John Stuart Mill, advocate that he was of "experiments in living" against the grain of Victorian morality. In Mill, liberalism's objective to break down old mental and social constraints, no less than legal ones, is quite clear. And in the nineteenth century, liberal foxes could not be certain of their project's success: they could brook no compromise of principle. This meant that liberal theory in the abstract could be taken much further than liberals themselves dared take it at the time. Mill was not an advocate of the strange new personal identities that have proliferated in the twen-

ty-first century, but his liberalism was preconceived to accommodate them, or almost anything else.

The two World Wars presented many new opportunities for psychological foxes, but the wars also entailed a renewed need for the
martial attributes and dependable loyalties of the lions. After each
conflict, many liberals redoubled their efforts to transform society, to
reclaim their position of overwhelming dominance and to stave off
the possibility of a turn toward a more leonine culture. War might be
disillusioning by itself, by why leave the outcome to uncertain nature,
when human effort can guarantee it?

The foxes fought a civil war with the lions, not with force—which
was not their *metier*, after all—but within the institutions of the
Western world, changing each institution's philosophy to favor their
side and to make institutions that were already favorable even more
so. The process unfolded from the schools to the press to government to the churches themselves. Only the Cold War checked the
advance a little: not only was there a need for lions to fight it, but the
principles on which it had to be fought could not be entirely liberal
ones. Traditional religion, in particular, was an indispensable ally, as
were loyalties to family and nation, both here at home and within
the Soviet bloc.

If it seems strange that Western foxes should have been willing to
resist the Soviet Union, as Cold War liberals did, two things must be
remembered. The first is of course that liberals throughout the Cold
War were divided between sympathizers and opponents of Soviet
Communism, with many of the opponents still perceiving the Western Right as a greater threat than the foreign power. The second thing
to recall is that the highly militarized Soviet Union was itself not a society in which foxes could flourish. A totalitarian yet business-minded
China, on the other hand, integrated within a "liberal international
order," was an altogether different proposition. After the Cold War,
the foxes of the West assumed that the fox-friendly ways of commerce
would inevitably lead China to liberalize, as the foxes there would

naturally gain the upper hand over militaristic lions in a world order defined by trade and loosened cultural ties.

This is not a Manichean story, and neither foxes nor lions are intrinsically good or bad. But the West became psychologically imbalanced, with one set of emotions and personality types predominating. Real human beings are never simply one type or another, and even in the most liberal society, people will feel drawn to defend the "persistence of aggregates" of some kind or another, in some degree. What the predominance of the psychological complex behind liberalism has led to, however, is the transformation of even the objects of lion-like devotion into liberal totems. The West today does not suffer only from an excess of cleverness—in fact, it suffers from sclerotic liberal stupidity as well, as ideas that were clever in their original contexts have become mere formulas and objects of blind loyalty. This accounts for the ironic complexity of the twenty-first-century Right, which includes foxes who have creatively rejected the "aggregates" of liberalism alongside those lions who still adhere to the values, traditions, and identities of the pre-liberal dispensation. The Left and center-Left—and, too often, what passes for the center-Right—is now itself the stupid party, lacking in innovative power even as it clings to the formulas of the innovators of yesteryear.

Even so, this decadent liberal Left has an easier task than the Right. To combine innovation and tradition, to reintegrate the lion with the fox, is much harder than to make an idol of a bygone spirit of novelty and freedom. The liberalism of today retains its poisonous character for the West, but has lost what creative power it once possessed. To purge the poison will however require creativity from conservatives, a thing that may sound simple enough but which in this case means going against psychological nature. Yet this is what is necessary if the West is to cease to be suicidal. Our nation and our civilization must have lions among its leaders, and foxes with the hearts of lions.

Contributors

———◆———

MICHAEL ANTON is a lecturer in politics and research fellow at Hillsdale College's Allan P. Kirby, Jr., Center for Constitutional Studies in Washington, D.C. He served on the National Security Council staff in the administrations of President George W. Bush and President Donald J. Trump and as speechwriter to Pete Wilson, Rudy Giuliani, Condoleezza Rice and Rupert Murdoch. He also spent twelve years in the private sector in corporate communications. His writings have appeared in *The Wall Street Journal*, *The Washington Post*, and the *Claremont Review of Books*, among many other publications.

DAVID AZERRAD is an assistant professor and research fellow at Hillsdale College's Van Andel Graduate School of Government in Washington, D.C. He was previously the director of the B. Kenneth Simon Center for Principles and Politics at The Heritage Foundation.

CHRISTOPHER BUSKIRK is the publisher and editor of *American Greatness*. He is a contributing opinion writer for *The New York Times*. He has written for *The Washington Post*, *The Spectator*, *USA Today*, *The Hill*, *The New Criterion*, and other publications. He is a frequent contributor to Fox News, NPR's Morning Edition, and the PBS Newshour. Chris is a sought-after speaker and has spoken recently at The Aspen Ideas Festival and to other groups around the country. He is the author of *Trump vs. The Leviathan* and the co-author of *American Greatness: How Conservatism, Inc. Missed the 2016 Election & What the Establishment Needs to Learn*. Chris is a serial entrepreneur who has built and sold businesses in financial services and digital marketing. He received his B.A. from Claremont McKenna College.

ANGELO M. CODEVILLA is professor emeritus of international relations at Boston University, a fellow of the Claremont Institute, and a member of the Hoover Institution's group on military history. He served on the staff of the Senate Intelligence Committee and on President Reagan's transition teams. He is the author of *The Character of Nations*, *War, Ends and Means*, and *To Make and Keep Peace*.

JOHN FONTE is a senior fellow at the Hudson Institute and the author of *Sovereignty or Submission: Will Americans Rule Themselves or be Ruled by Others?* (Encounter), winner of the Intercollegiate Studies Institute book award for 2012 and a number-one Amazon best-seller in international law. He has been appointed by the President and confirmed by the Senate to serve on the National Council of the Humanities.

VICTOR DAVIS HANSON is a senior fellow at the Hoover Institution, Stanford University, and the author of *The Second World Wars* (Basic Books), as well as *Carnage and Culture*, *A War Like No Other*, and *The Savior Generals*.

ROGER KIMBALL is editor and publisher of *The New Criterion* and president and publisher of Encounter Books. He writes regular columns at *American Greatness*, *The Spectator (U.S. Edition)*, and *The Epoch Times*. His latest book is *The Fortunes of Permanence: Culture and Anarchy in an Age of Amnesia*.

DANIEL MCCARTHY is the editor of *Modern Age: A Conservative Review* and the director of the Robert Novak Journalism Fellowship Program at the Fund for American Studies. He is also a columnist for *The Spectator* (U.S. Edition) and serves on the advisory board of the Edmund Burke Foundation.

JAMES PIERESON is a senior fellow at The Manhattan Institute and the President of the William E. Simon Foundation. He is the author of *Shattered Consensus* (2015) and *Camelot and the Cultural Revolution* (2007), both published by Encounter Books. He has contributed essays and reviews to numerous publications, including *The New Criterion, Commentary, The Wall Street Journal, National Review*, and *The Washington Post.*

JOHN O'SULLIVAN is president and founder of the Danube Institute in Budapest; international editor of *Quadrant Magazine* in Sydney, Australia; associate editor of the *Hungarian Review*, a fellow of the National Review Institute; and an editor at large of *National Review*. He is a co-founder and director of Twenty-First Century Initiatives, as well as co-founder of the International Reagan Thatcher Society.

Index